Tea Room

For as long as I can remember, a cup of tea has been the beverage that brings us together and I love the many rituals and ceremonies we have cultivated around it. Tea gathers us around kitchen tables, office desks and fancy restaurant tables. It helps the conversation to flow, and allows us to enjoy the company of others whilst savouring its sweetness. During difficult times, we offer a cup of tea as solace; for celebrations, a tea party is always a popular choice. Tea fits all occasions, all ages, and has a flavour to suit all tastes.

For this issue of YARN, we found inspiration in the tastes, colours and origins of four of my favourite tea flavours: 'English Tea' with its rich traditions; Oolong, elegant and exquisite like Asia itself; Ginger and Saffron with their Eastern zing and Matcha, at the moment the trendiest of them all.

We're treating you to lots of garments in this issue. The Nishio Sweater on p.12 is a very special sweater as it resembles knitwear, but it's crocheted and inspired by the linear patterns and textures seen on Matcha plantations. The Jasmine Poncho (with detachable cowl) on p.52 was a firm favourite in our office with ladies of all shapes and sizes, passing it around enthusiastically to be sampled (with everyone adding their own twist on styling!). Another beautiful garment is the Qing Xin Sweater on p.46 with its striking silhouette.

During the production of this issue we've been in conversations with an anthropologist and graduates from two Universities (Amsterdam and Leiden) in both Cultural Analysis and Japanese Studies, and with an Asia Consultant from Machi Consulting to ensure we have been mindful, respectful and educated in the cultures surrounding the teas we've been inspired by.

So pour yourself a large cup of tea. Add a little milk, lemon or honey and take your time to 'leaf' through the pages of Tea Room and be inspired to create something wonderful.

Put the kettle on

Nothing stands the test of time better than tea. With the ever changing nature of tea blends and their creative packaging, Tea Rooms are continuing sources of inspiration. Tea never goes out of fashion, constantly reflecting the spirit of each generation. So join us as we embark on a journey through our favourite flavours of tea.

CONTENTS

COMMISSIONED BY

scheepjes.com

CONCEPT, STYLING & ART DIRECTION
Marita Janssen
GRAPHIC DESIGN
Suzanne Nuis
CREATIVE DIRECTORS SCHEEPJES
Anita Mundt & Simy Somer
MANAGING EDITOR
Christa Veenstra
TEXT, TRANSLATION AND EDITING
Kirsten Ballering, Esme Crick,
Flory Hartog, Henrieke Schuiling
ILLUSTRATIONS
Henrieke Schuiling
PHOTOGRAPHY
Violaine Chappallaz, Dana van Leeuwen
Ernst Yperlaan, Unsplash, Stocksy
MAKE-UP ARTISTS
Corinne van der Heijden, Djolien de Kreij
MODELS
Billy, Tilly-Euromodels, Nour-EvD agency,
Roderick and Catherine-Special Max
DESIGNERS
Jellina Verhoeff, Amanda Beaumont,
Martin Up North, Susan Walsh,
Margje Enting, Tatsiana Kupryianchyk,
Maria McPherson, Nerissa Muijs,
Christa Veenstra, Johanna Lindahl,
Carmen Jorissen, Ana D,
Rachele Carmona, Margaret Hubert,
Alia Bland

FOR INQUIRIES ABOUT YARN
creative@scheepjes.com
Mercuriusweg 16, 9482 WL Tynaarlo
The Netherlands

Language: Dutch and English
Publication: twice a year
ISBN 9789491840463
© 2019

This little icon indicates
the relevant page number
for the instructions for
each design. The pattern
book starts on page 61.

04 MATCHA
06 LEAVES SCARF
08 CHASEN BEANIE
10 SOULSTORM BLANKET
12 NISHIO SWEATER

14 SAFFRON & GINGER
16 GINGER ROOT GLOVES
18 HONEY PONCHO
20 SAFFRON WRAP
22 SPICE MARKET SNOOD

32 ENGLISH TEA
34 BLOOMING TEA COSY
36 PETALS & LEAVES SHAWL
38 EARL GREY SOCKS
40 LADY MABEL SWEATER

44 OOLONG
46 QING XIN SWEATER
50 OOLONG BLANKET
52 JASMINE PONCHO WITH COWL
54 ORCHARD BLOSSOM HEADBAND

61 PATTERN BOOK

IN THIS ISSUE:
24 INSPIRING ARTIST: RUBY SILVIOUS
26 INSPIRING ARTIST: DAGMAR STAP
28 10X TEA ROOMS OF THE WORLD
42 SIMY'S CHALLENGE
56 ROZETA CROCHET-A-LONG
58 SCHEEPJES BLOGGER: MARIA MCPHERSON
60 NAMASTE TRAIN CASE

MATCHA

LEAVES SCARF
BY JELLINA VERHOEFF

All eyes on green! This lush,
two-toned scarf comes in a generous
length which allows you to wrap yourself
in the essence of matcha.

SCHEEPJES STONE WASHED

62

CHASEN BEANIE

BY AMANDA BEAUMONT

Hoodie, raincoat and trousers **uniqlo.com**

Inspired by a traditional Japanese
matcha whisk, the Chasen, this comfortable
beanie will embrace your head
and keep it snug.

SCHEEPJES STONE WASHED XL

65

SOULSTORM
BLANKET

BY MARTIN UP NORTH

The mesmerising labyrinth of stitches creates an eye-catching centrepiece for your bedroom.

SCHEEPJES CAHLISTA

64

NISHIO SWEATER

BY SUSAN WALSH

68

Express your love by creating a handmade garment. This crocheted sweater, inspired by the Japanese matcha fields of Nishio, makes the perfect gift.

SCHEEPJES OUR TRIBE

SAFFRON AND GINGER

Ginger Root Gloves

BY MARGJE ENTING

The change of season welcomes a change of accessories.
These comfortable and practical fingerless gloves feature
traditional stranded colourwork designs in spicy tones.

SCHEEPJES METROPOLIS

72

You are my
favourite cup
of Tea

As honey is to tea, this poncho is comfort food for your soul.
Rich and warm, adorned with delicate droplets, this will be your
go-to garment of the season.

SCHEEPJES MERINO SOFT BRUSH

Honey PONCHO

BY TATSIANA KUPRYIANCHYK

Jumper uniqlo.com, trousers tally-ho.nl

Saffron Wrap

BY MARIA MCPHERSON

Just as the smallest flake of saffron transforms a meal, tiny beads transform this golden wrap into a luxurious accessory.

SCHEEPJES WHIRL OMBRÉ

80

Spice Market Snood

BY NERISSA MUIJS

The flavours of India have inspired this textured, oversized snood.
Envelop yourself in the warmth of this statement piece.

SCHEEPJES NAMASTE

74

A CUP OF
ART

Artworks so small they can easily fit into the palm of your hand:
Ruby Silvious' miniature paintings on the delicate paper of used,
dried tea bags are very special indeed. 'Black tea and Rooibos tea
create beautiful dark stains that give a tea bag character.'

RUBY SILVIOUS, ARTIST

'About five years ago, I was having tea with my sister and we came up with the idea of making designs with tea leaves. Our experiment failed, dramatically I might add, but the thought of doing something with used tea stuck in my mind. That's when I decided to use tea bags instead of tea leaves to create my art.' Since she discovered this unusual canvas, Ruby has painted hundreds of miniature paintings on used, dried tea bags. She has mastered the art of emptying out the old tea leaves ('I watch my favourite series on Netflix while doing this') before drying the bags, and knows exactly which tea varieties create the best stains to add an extra dimension to her paintings: 'Black tea and Rooibos tea leave beautiful, dark stains. They give character to the paper, and create a used and worn feel. Tea with turmeric gives the bags a deep, mustard yellow colour resembling a warm sunrise. Some teas, hibiscus and forest fruit for example, leave a beautiful bluish hue.'

'My mood, whereabouts, and meal choices all determine my choice of tea. In Japan I usually prefer green tea; at home I drink English Breakfast or a similar black tea'

TINY AND DELICATE

Ruby's most impressive work could well be her inspired project to create a tea bag painting every day, for 363 consecutive days. 'I believe this is my greatest achievement to date. These works have been combined into a single book. A dream come true.' Reused materials always form the basis of her work. 'I am an artist who repurposes discarded materials. I turn everyday objects into works of art. I believe that by creating art with unconventional materials, I can spark creativity and challenge people to think about the world around them.' Her own work rarely ends up in the recycling bin. 'In my studio I have many boxes filled with experiments- monoprints, tea bags, pastel drawings and illustrations- all waiting to be reused. Most of these creations earn a spot in one of my sketchbooks or become part of a collage, so nothing is ever lost.' Does this New York artist create larger works as well? 'Yes, I sure do, although I prefer the miniature dimensions, say three by six centimetres. A mini canvas makes me feel as if I have more control over the painting, and it easily fits into my pocket. I can take it with me and paint anywhere I want, whenever I feel like it.'

rubysilvious.com

Embroidery is
MINDFULNESS

Two years ago, Dagmar Stap picked up an embroidery needle, made an exact copy of a Chicken Yum Yum package and knew instantly: this was it. For YARN, she has embroidered a Pukka tea box to fit with this issue's theme. 'What an intense experience. The packaging of this product has so much going on'.

DAGMAR STAP, ARTIST

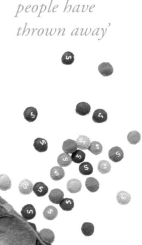

'I'm always searching for new packaging, tempted to dive into any bin to discover what people have thrown away'

Embroidery? At first, she thought it was rather old-school and frumpy, but in fact it offered Dagmar the medium that she'd been searching for- at that time, she was studying illustration at Academie Minerva, a Dutch art academy- so she decided to give it a go. She embroidered the image from a package onto felt and was hooked immediately. 'Embroidery is quite easy to learn. From the outset, I didn't limit myself to particular stitches, and that gave me a lot of freedom to adopt my own style very quickly.' Where does this fascination for packaging come from? 'Before I took up embroidery, I used to paint and draw packages. I particularly like examples with lots of illustrations on them, so it won't be a surprise when I tell you I love going to Asian supermarkets. Some of the packaging there is really eye-catching. Oh, and I also like the thick, bold lettering. And colour, lots of colour,' she laughs. 'Anything loud, really.'

SLOW DOWN

Embroidered packages that perfectly resemble the original add an extra layer to the underlying concept of packaging, says Dagmar: 'Packaging protects your food. You take the food out, and throw the container away. It's a very fleeting product, a hasty, throw-away item: the continuous cycle of production and consumption. At the same time, good packaging requires a thoughtful design process. Experts have thought carefully about the use of colour, typography, target audience, the right look and feel. It's an artwork in itself. I try to capture this with a needle and thread and slow down the sense of haste. The methodical technique of embroidery fits this concept well and gives the package texture, contrary to the original smooth, plastic surface feel.'

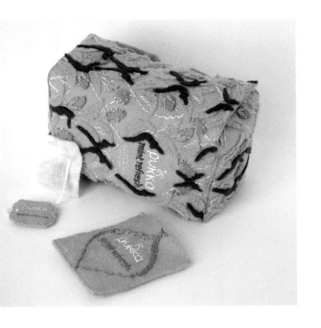

IT'S ALL IN THE DETAIL

The added benefit of beautiful packaging is the contents. After all, you eat or drink what's inside. And no, a beautiful exterior does not always guarantee a beautiful interior. Dagmar still shudders when she remembers a carton of melon milk she once opened: 'It was horrible! And it had this fluorescent green colour that should have made my alarm bells go off... Skittles have the opposite effect. I love them!' The true reward lies in the time and energy she puts into her embroidery projects. 'I try to put in as much detail as possible, so the end results reflect my efforts. Embroidery brings me inner peace and focus, and that's what I love about it most of all. It's an opportunity to completely immerse myself and concentrate fully on that specific package. At a wonderfully slow pace, no need to rush. And when I've completed my work, I love it when the beauty of packaging grabs someone's attention and makes them think, 'Hey, that's interesting'.'

10× TEA ROOMS

OUR SELECTION OF THE WORLD'S FINEST
TEA ROOMS: SOME ARE MODERN AND MINIMALIST.
OTHERS HAVE CLASSIC INTERIORS OF GRANDEUR
TAKING YOU BACK TO BYGONE DAYS.

1.

1 HUXINTING TEA HOUSE
SHANGHAI, CHINA
This impressive pavilion on stilts (dating back to the Ming dynasty) is a feast for both eyes and taste buds. People have been flocking here since 1855 to enjoy traditional Chinese tea and snacks.
• chinatravel.com/shanghai-attraction/huxinting-tea-house/

2 P&T TEA STORE
BERLIN, GERMANY
What do you get when you combine fine tea and beautiful art objects with a minimalist interior? That's right: a tea temple where the stress of daily life slips away as soon as you enter.
• paperandtea.com

3 BETTYS
AT 6 LOCATIONS IN YORKSHIRE, UK
The quintessence of English charm, Bettys has been a great success ever since it opened in 1919. All six branches evoke an impression of tea grandeur: the shop, finest tea blends, lovely snacks as well as starched table linen all exude British excellence.
• bettys.co.uk

4 PUERH BROOKLYN
NEW YORK, US
At the heart of New York's trendy Williamsburg district, Puerh offers a bold and peaceful interior where you can enjoy more than twenty different Puerhs (fermented tea from Yunnan, southwest China) and other tea blends.
• puerhbrooklyn.com

5 BETJEMAN & BARTON
THE HAGUE, THE NETHERLANDS
Founded by Englishman Arthur Betjeman and Frenchman Percy Barton, this tea house celebrates its centenary this year and offers tea lovers a perfect mix of classic English and frivolous French styles.
• betjemanandbarton.nl

6 SAMOVAR

SAN FRANCISCO, US

Samovar stands for slow living: (herbal) tea, healthy food, and a serene setting guarantee relaxation and awareness.

• samovartea.com

7 MARIAGE FRÈRES

PARIS, FRANCE

A tea salon which truly values tradition and prestige. Relax in one of their antique chairs and breathe in the atmosphere of bygone times, while savouring one of the refined tea blends on offer.

• mariagefreres.com

8 SKETCH

LONDON, UK

This London studio once belonged to Christian Dior. Today, visitors can treat themselves to wonderful tea blends and delicacies, in a remarkable interior decked out in wall-to-wall pink. Don't forget to visit the quirky restroom where the toilets are hidden inside egg-shaped pods.

• sketch.london

9 GREAT WALL TEA

NEW WESTMINSTER, CANADA

Although the mosaic wall of tea tins catches your eye when you enter, this modern tea bar is in fact known for its great selection of top quality, fresh leaf tea.

• facebook.com/GreatWallTea/

10 TO TSAI

ATHENS, GREECE

A tea restaurant/shop with a serene and minimalist light wood interior which gives it an almost Scandinavian feel. The perfect place to escape the busy city and enjoy a heart-warming cup of (herbal) tea.

• tea.gr

WE ♥ TEA

This top-10 is our selection, but no doubt there are many more beautiful, interesting and unique Tea Rooms out there. Share your favourite tea address on Instagram using #scheepjeslovestea.

English
TEA

BLOOMING
Tea Cosy
BY CHRISTA VEENSTRA

Like the details on your most treasured bone china teacup,
this crocheted tea cosy is a delight from every angle.

SCHEEPJES CATONA

Petals & Leaves
SHAWL

BY JOHANNA LINDAHL

Luxury and romance are
a match made in heaven.
Echoing floral patterns, this
lace work shawl is enhanced
by an ombré colour effect.

SCHEEPJES WHIRLIGIG

84

EARL GREY

Socks

BY CARMEN JORISSEN

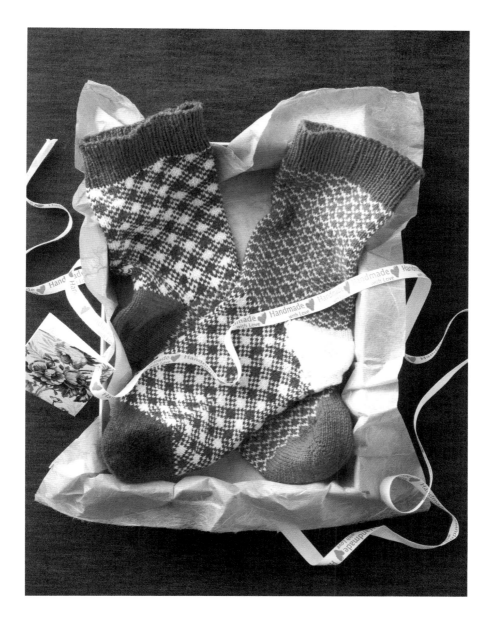

Add a little eccentricity to your look with these quirky knitted socks.
Combine colours with the patterns in various ways to give them personality.

SCHEEPJES METROPOLIS

86

Lady Mabel SWEATER

BY SUSAN WALSH

Crochet masquerading as knitting, this is a 'proper' sweater with beautiful cable detailling.
It's sure to become a staple of every wardrobe.

SCHEEPJES OUR TRIBE

88

Skirt **wefashion.nl**, glasses **dragon**

Simy's
CHALLENGE

Upcycling

If you are anything like me, you can't resist the allure of a thrift store. On those rare occasions when I have time, or when I'm travelling and find myself in a new destination, an afternoon spent wandering around the local thrift stores is always a pleasure.

Amongst the bone china mismatched teacups and saucers, and a wealth of other discarded treasures, I often come across the most beautiful knitted items. The passing of time and changing fashions may have turned them into yesterday's must-haves, but a lovingly hand knitted sweater or a 100% woollen blanket is a nugget of gold waiting to be found.

In today's era of slow fashion and eco awareness, upcycling is enjoying quite a renaissance. To take something that has been cast aside, neglected or unloved, and make it into a useable item is a skill, and for many people, a passion.

These hand warmers were created by my good friend and fellow thrift store stalker Susan from the wonderful Felted Button blog (feltedbutton.com). She decided to indulge in a really handmade look while creating them. Lucky enough to find two perfect sweaters at her local thrift store (the colours and patterns spoke to her), she snipped, stitched, styled and decorated to create something new and unique!

Any woollen item can be felted- simply pop it in the washing machine on a hot and vigorous wash and wait to see the results. It's an art form more than a science, so the end results are often a surprise.

So, if you are waiting for permission to spend an afternoon perusing your local thrift store, here it is! Enjoy the process of creating something new from your finds and upload the end results to social media with #SimysChallenge so I, and others, can see and be inspired by your upcycled creations.

Happy Hunting!

Oolong

Qing Xin

SWEATER

BY ANA D

This boxed sleeve sweater gives complete freedom of movement. The juxtaposition of two contrasting stitch patterns lends subtle details to this garment, inspired by the oolong growing region of Qing Xin. The yarn used is single spun and twisted in a similar way to how the leaves of oolong tea are rolled.

SCHEEPJES NAMASTE

95

*Tea
is the elixir
of Life*

LAO TZU

OOLONG
Blanket

BY RACHELE CARMONA

Reminiscent of aged wooden
panelling, this weighty blanket
is decorated with surface crochet
and matching tassels.

SCHEEPJES STONE WASHED XL

94

JASMINE PONCHO
BY MARGARET HUBERT
With Cowl

Versatility is the strength of this soft, single-sleeved garment. Its asymmetric form is ideal for creating serene layers, and the separate cowl gives it endless styling options.

SCHEEPJES METROPOLIS

96

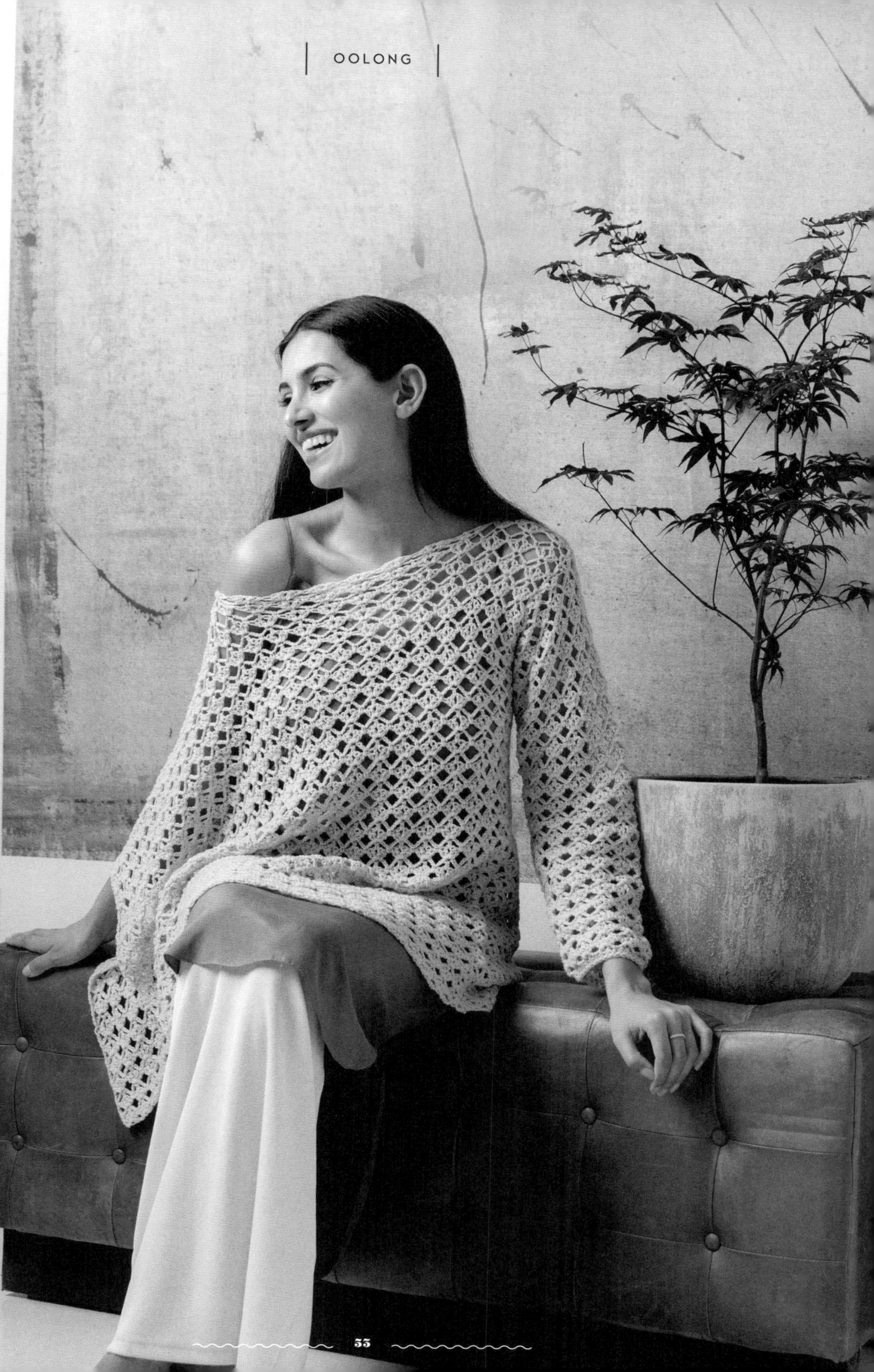

Tunic and dress **cosstores.com**

Upcycled tunic episode.eu

Orchard Blossom
HEADBAND
BY ALIA BLAND

Whatever your activity, whether it's running, yoga, cycling, or simply going
out for tea with friends, this headband will mix and match with your active lifestyle.

SCHEEPJES ELIZA AND CAHLISTA

98

ROZETA
CAL

BY TATSIANA KUPRYIANCHYK

Join us in creating this beautiful blanket over 11 weeks supported by
pdf patterns, video tutorials and the Scheepjes Facebook group community.
Inspired by rose windows found in gothic architecture, silhouetted
against the sky at different times of day.

Crochet-A-Long

Dawn

Twilight

Dusk

Midnight

PROJECT SUPPORT:
facebook.com/groups/ScheepjesCAL.International/

FOR MORE INFORMATION:
scheepjes.com/RozetaCAL-EN

MARIA McPHERSON

Who Maria McPherson (51)
Blog Fifty Shades of 4 Ply
Arts and crafts? 'I've been
enjoying arts and crafts for as
long as I can remember. My
mother always gave me arts
and crafts kits for Christmas,
so I learned at an early age.
I've done almost everything,
from candle making to painting.'
Spotlight? 'I prefer to stay
below the radar. I don't like
being the centre of attention!'

*'I'm left-handed;
that's why my
knitting techniques
are a bit quirky'*

Inspiration

'I find inspiration pretty much everywhere.
In exceptional design, vintage curtains, and
Mother Nature's wonderful colour combinations.
I like being outdoors, out in the countryside.
I live in Northumberland, England, which neigh-
bours the Scottish Borders, and I'm surrounded
by areas of exceptional natural beauty.
It's such an inspirational region, all the way
from the coast to beyond the hill tops. The local
St Abbs Wool Festival is held here twice a year.
I always try to attend. The festival supports local
businesses and offers a wide range of products,
from yarn to fabrics. What do I like about arts
and crafts? There's always something new to
learn. Currently high on my personal to-learn-list
are colourwork and Fair Isle knitting projects.'

DESIGNS IN
PREVIOUS
ISSUES OF
YARN

SIGNATURE

'My designs are relatively easy to make, never really complicated. They're perfect for beginners, and are fun projects to take on while watching television. By combining a clever use of colours and straightforward design, I'm able to produce a special end result. My favourite design is my Kizzy blanket, a traditional granny square project with a broad, lacy border. I made it using Scheepjes River Washed yarn. The colour combination always brings a smile to my face. I've been enjoying arts and crafts for as long as I can remember. When I was young, my mother gave me all kinds of arts and craft kits for Christmas, every year. I'm a self-taught knitter. My style is rather quirky as I'm left-handed! I didn't take up crocheting until much later, with the help of a very patient friend and a helpful book for left-handed creatives. My first attempts were hilarious, but I always succeeded in the end! Today I focus on knitting, crocheting and spinning.'

MY CUP OF TEA

'I drink tea every day. Indeed, usually the first thing I do when I get up in the morning is treat myself to a nice, hot cuppa. I keep it simple: a cup of English Breakfast tea, regular black tea that is, with a dash of semi-skimmed milk. That's it. No sweet, fruity flavours, no thank you. And although I'm English, I actually prefer tea bags over loose tea leaves. I'm too impatient for that. I also drink coffee by the way, but I try to limit my intake to two cups a day. Too much caffeine gives me the jitters. Do I like something sweet with my tea? Well, I try not to make a habit of it, but occasionally I love to treat myself to a slice of lemon cake.'

COLOUR: BLUSH. ITEM NO. 64963

NAMASTE TRAIN CASE

WHEN CREATIVITY
AND PRACTICALITY
MEET MINDFULNESS,
THEY BRING MOMENTS
OF PEACE AND HAPPINESS
WHEN YOU'RE CRAFTING
ON THE MOVE.

This vintage style crafter's case is made with travel in mind. Covered in
vegan leather, this must-have accessory is consciously produced.
Attention to detail creates ease of use with an integrated U-shaped yarn feeder
(so you can craft away and keep your items safely stored inside), and magnets
in the lid for storing pins and needles for quick and easy access.

PATTERN
BOOK

For each pattern in this Pattern book the skill level is indicated with 1, 2 or 3 leaves. 1 leaf indicates easy, 3 leaves indicates it's a design for the more advanced crafter.

LEAVES SCARF
By Jellina Verhoeff
jellina-creations.nl

MEASUREMENTS
176 x 27cm (69.3 x 10.5in)

ABBREVIATIONS
See back cover flap

MATERIALS
Scheepjes Stone Washed (78% Cotton, 22% Acrylic; 50g/130m)
Yarn A: 825 Malachite x 4 balls
Yarn B: 827 Peridot x 4 balls
4.5mm crochet hook

GAUGE/TENSION
18 sts and 21 rows to measure 10 x 10cm over dc using a 4.5mm hook.

SPECIAL ABBREVIATIONS
dcA double crochet with Yarn A
dcB double crochet with Yarn B

PATTERN NOTES
With tapestry crochet, carry unused yarn along as you work, trapping it inside sts worked in main colour, and switch colours to create patterns. Trap unused yarn in the back of each st as you go.
Colour change always happens in st before switch as folls: insert hook into st, yoh, pull through in old colour, yoh in new colour, and pull through. Turn work after each row.

INSTRUCTIONS

With Yarn A, ch50. Join Yarn B.
Row 1 With Yarn A, ch1 (does not count as st throughout), 1dcA in second ch from hook, 9dcA, (10dcB, 10dcA) twice, turn. [50 dc]
Row 2 Ch1, (10dcB, 10dcA) twice, 10dcB, turn.

Row 3 Ch1, 1dcB, (8dcA, 5dcB, 2dcA, 5dcB) twice, 8dcA, 1dcB.
Row 4 Ch1, 1dcA, (8dcA, 5dcA, 2dcB, 5dcA) twice, 8dcB, 1dcA.
Row 5 Ch1, 2dcB, (6dcA, 5dcB, 4dcA, 5dcB) twice, 6dcA, 2dcB.
Row 6 Ch1, 2dcA, (6dcB, 5dcA, 4dcB, 5dcA) twice, 6dcB, 2dcA.
Row 7 Ch1, 3dcB, (4dcA, 5dcB, 6dcA, 5dcB) twice, 4dcA, 3dcB.
Row 8 Ch1, 3dcA, (4dcB, 5dcA, 6dcB, 5dcA) twice, 4dcB, 3dcA.
Row 9 Ch1, 4dcB, (2dcA, 5dcB, 8dcA, 5dcB) twice, 2dcA, 4dcB.
Row 10 Ch1, 4dcA, (2dcB, 5dcA, 8dcB, 5dcA) twice, 2dcB, 4dcA.
Row 11 Rep Row 2.
Row 12 Rep Row 1.
Row 13 Rep Row 2.
Row 14 Rep Row 1.
Row 15 Rep Row 9.
Row 16 Rep Row 10.
Row 17 Rep Row 7.
Row 18 Rep Row 8.
Row 19 Rep Row 5.
Row 20 Rep Row 6.
Row 21 Rep Row 3.
Row 22 Rep Row 4.
Row 23 Rep Row 1.
Row 24 Rep Row 2.
Rows 25-312 Rep Rows 1-24 a further 12 times.

TO FINISH
Fasten off and weave in ends.

STITCH CHART 1: STITCH PATTERN
Note: Remember to work colour change in last step of last st in prev colour for EVERY colour change (not marked in patt), and at end of every row, except Rows 2 and 22.

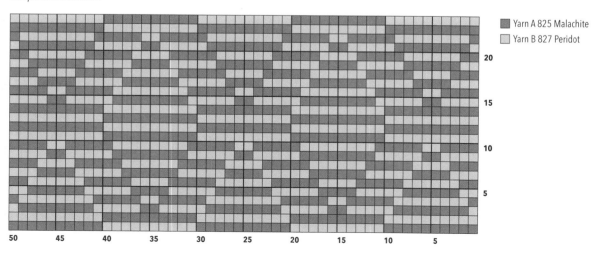

■ Yarn A 825 Malachite
□ Yarn B 827 Peridot

CHASEN BEANIE
By Amanda Beaumont
thecalmnookcrafts.blogspot.com

MEASUREMENTS
22cm wide x 20cm high (8.5 x 7.8in)
flat and unblocked
28cm wide x 22cm high (11 x 8.5in)
flat and blocked

ABBREVIATIONS
See back cover flap

MATERIALS
Scheepjes Stone Washed XL (70% Cotton, 30% Acrylic; 50g/75m)
Yarn A: 865 Malachite x 2 balls
Yarn B: 866 Fosterite x 1 ball
5mm circular needle, 40cm long
5.5mm circular needle, 40cm long
5.5mm circular needle, 80cm long (if using magic loop method) or set
of 5.5mm dpn's for crown decreases
Cable needle

GAUGE/TENSION
16 sts and 24 rows to measure 10 x 10cm in st st in the round using
5.5mm needles (unblocked).
24 sts and 24 rows to measure 10 x 10cm in cabled patt in the round
using 5.5mm needles (unblocked).

SPECIAL ABBREVIATIONS
C4F four-stitch front cable: slip next 2 sts onto cable needle, hold them
at front of work, k2 from left hand needle, k2 from cable needle

PATTERN NOTES
The needle sizes are a guide. Different sized needles may be needed to
meet required gauge.
This patt can be adjusted by adding or subtracting multiples of 6 sts
and by repeating Rounds 6-10 more/fewer times. All crown decreases
remain the same, regardless of any size modifications.
All knit sts are worked in Yarn A and purl sts in Yarn B, unless stated
otherwise.
When using two yarns, carry yarn in the same way throughout. In this
patt, Yarn A was carried under Yarn B. Be aware of float tension, making
sure to spread sts out as you go to ensure hat has enough stretch and
will not be bunched up.
When decreasing at the crown, the sts will not fit comfortably around
40cm long circular needle: change to 80cm circular needle and use
magic loop method or change to dpn's if preferred.

INSTRUCTIONS

With Yarn A, 5mm circular needle and long tail cast-on method, cast on
108 sts.
Pm to denote beg of round, being careful not to twist sts, join to work
in the round.
Rounds 1-5 *K1, p1; rep from * to end of round.

BODY OF HAT
Join Yarn B, do not fasten off Yarn A.

Round 1 K1 in Yarn B, *k4 in Yarn A, k2 in Yarn B; rep from * to last
5 sts, k4 in Yarn A, k1 in Yarn B.
Change to 5.5mm circular needle.
Note: Now use Yarn B for all purl sts unless instructed otherwise.
Rounds 2-4 P1, *k4, p2; rep from * to last st, p1.
Round 5 P1, *C4F, p2; rep from * to last 5 sts, C4F, p1.
Rounds 6-9 P1, *k4, p2; rep from * to last st, p1.
Round 10 P1, *C4F, p2; rep from * to last 5 sts, C4F, p1.
Rounds 6-10 form patt, rep these rounds 4 more times.

CROWN DECREASES
Round 1 P1, *k4, p2; rep from * to last 5 sts, k4, p1.
Round 2 P1, *k2tog, k2, p2; rep from * to last 5 sts, k2tog, k2, p1.
[90 sts]
Round 3 P1, *k3, p2; rep from * to last 4 sts, k3, p1.
Round 4 P1, *k2tog, k1, p2; rep from * to last 4 sts, k2tog, k1, p1.
[72 sts]
Round 5 P1, *k2, p2; rep from * to last 3 sts, k2, p1, rm, slip last st
worked back to left needle, pm, this is the new beg of round.
Round 6 *K2tog in Yarn B, k2 in Yarn A; rep from * to end. [54 sts]
Round 7 *K1 in Yarn B, k2 in Yarn A; rep from * to end.
Round 8 *K1 in Yarn B, k2tog in Yarn A; rep from * to end. [36 sts]
Round 9 *K1 in Yarn B, k1 in Yarn A; rep from * to end.
Fasten off Yarn B leaving tail to weave in.
Round 10 K2tog to end. [18 sts]
Round 11 K to end.
Round 12 K2tog to end. [9 sts]
Fasten off leaving a 25cm tail.

TO FINISH
Thread yarn tail onto tapestry needle and slip thread through rem sts,
pull tightly to close circle on crown of hat. Weave in ends.
Wash, block and dry hat. If required, block damp hat over a blown-up
balloon to create shape.

SOULSTORM BLANKET
By Martin Up North
martinupnorthblog.wordpress.com

MEASUREMENTS
135 x 190cm (53.3 x 74.8in)
after blocking

ABBREVIATIONS
See back cover flap

MATERIALS
Scheepjes Cahlista (100% Natural Cotton; 50g/85m)
Yarn A: 515 Emerald x 27 balls
Yarn B: 124 Ultramarine x 24 balls
5mm crochet hook

GAUGE/TENSION
15 sts and 19 rows to measure 10 x 10cm over patt using a 5mm hook.

SPECIAL ABBREVIATIONS
cc colour change: work last dc of row in old colour up to final 2 lps on hook, draw through new colour to finish st. Leave yarn not in use hanging at side of work
mtr mosaic treble crochet: 1tr in skipped st two rows below, worked *in front* of ch-sps below

PATTERN NOTES
The first dc is always worked in same st as ch1 at end of prev row. Ch1 does not count as a st.
Each ch-2 sp counts as 1 st, so where instructed to skip 1 st at a ch-2 sp, skip that ch-2 sp.
Keep both yarns attached unless instructed otherwise, and pick up yarn used two rows below as required to alternate between colours. Turn after each row.
Patt is adjustable to a multiple of (48 ch) plus 4 ch for starting ch.

CHART PATTERN NOTES
Each chart row represents **two** rows worked in same colour, so each square represents two rows and 1 st per row. The first row of a colour creates patt, the second row reinforces it. The second row of a colour is worked with 1dc in every dc or mtr, and ch2 over every ch-2 sp. Follow chart from bottom to top and from right to left. First (and last) square in a row determines which colour to use for these two rows. Where a Yarn B st appears in a Yarn A row (and vice versa), ch2 and skip 1 st. Mtr is always worked into the same colour 'skipped st' 2 rows below. Chart is repeated 4 times in width and 4 times in length to achieve measurements given.

INSTRUCTIONS

With Yarn A, ch196.
Row 1 (RS) 1dc in second ch from hook and in each ch to end, ch1, turn. [195 dc]
Row 2 (WS) 1dc in each st to end, cc to Yarn B, ch1, turn.
Row 3 1dc, *ch2, skip 1 st, 23dc; rep from * 7 more times, ch2, skip 1 st, 1dc, ch1.
Row 4 1dc, *ch2, skip 1 st, 23dc; rep from * 7 more times, ch2, skip 1 st, 1dc, cc to Yarn A, ch1.
Row 5 1dc, *1mtr, ch2, skip 1 st, 21dc, ch2, skip 1 st; rep from * 7 more times, 1mtr, 1dc, ch1.
Row 6 1dc, *1dc, ch2, skip 1 st, 21dc, ch2, skip 1 st; rep from * 7 more times, 2dc, cc, ch1.
Row 7 1dc, *ch2, skip 1 st, 1mtr, ch2, skip 1 st, 19dc, ch2, skip 1 st, 1mtr; rep from * 7 more times, ch2, skip 1 st, 1dc, ch1.
Row 8 1dc, *ch2, skip 1 st, 1dc, ch2, skip 1 st, 19dc, ch2, skip 1 st, 1dc; rep from * 7 more times, ch2, skip 1 st, 1dc, cc, ch1.
Row 9 1dc, *(1mtr, ch2, skip 1 st) twice, 17dc, ch2, skip 1 st, 1mtr, ch2, skip 1 st; rep from * 7 more times, 1mtr, 1dc, ch1.
Row 10 1dc, *(1dc, ch2, skip 1 st) twice, 17dc, ch2, skip 1 st, 1dc, ch2, skip 1 st; rep from * 7 more times, 2dc, cc, ch1.
Row 11 1dc, *(ch2, skip 1 st, 1mtr) twice, ch2, skip 1 st, 15dc, (ch2, skip 1 st, 1mtr) twice; rep from * 7 more times, ch2, skip 1 st, 1dc, ch1.
Row 12 1dc, *(ch2, skip 1 st, 1dc) twice, ch2, skip 1 st, 15dc, (ch2, skip 1 st, 1dc) twice; rep from * 7 more times, ch2, skip 1 st, 1dc, cc, ch1.
Row 13 1dc, *(1mtr, ch2, skip 1 st) 3 times, 13dc, (ch2, skip 1 st, 1mtr) twice, ch2, skip 1 st; rep from * 7 more times, 1mtr, 1dc, ch1.
Row 14 1dc, *(1dc, ch2, skip 1 st) 3 times, 13dc, (ch2, skip 1 st, 1dc) twice, ch2, skip 1 st; rep from * 7 more times, 2dc, cc, ch1.
Row 15 1dc, *(ch2, skip 1 st, 1mtr) 3 times, ch2, skip 1 st, 11dc, (ch2, skip 1 st, 1mtr) 3 times; rep from * 7 more times, ch2, skip 1 st, 1dc, ch1.
Row 16 1dc, *(ch2, skip 1 st, 1dc) 3 times, ch2, skip 1 st, 11dc, (ch2, skip 1 st, 1dc) 3 times; rep from * 7 more times, ch2, skip 1 st, 1dc, cc, ch1.
Row 17 1dc, *(1mtr, ch2, skip 1 st) 4 times, 9dc, (ch2, skip 1 st, 1mtr) 3 times, ch2, skip 1 st; rep from * 7 more times, 1mtr, 1dc, ch1.
Row 18 1dc, *(1dc, ch2, skip 1 st) 4 times, 9dc, (ch2, skip 1 st, 1dc) 3 times, ch2, skip 1 st; rep from * 7 more times, 2dc, cc, ch1.
Row 19 1dc, *(ch2, skip 1 st, 1mtr) 4 times, ch2, skip 1 st, 7dc, (ch2, skip 1 st, 1mtr) 4 times; rep from * 7 more times, ch2, skip 1 st, 1dc, ch1.
Row 20 1dc, *(ch2, skip 1 st, 1dc) 4 times, ch2, skip 1 st, 7dc, (ch2, skip 1 st, 1dc) 4 times; rep from * 7 more times, ch2, skip 1 st, 1dc, cc, ch1.
Row 21 1dc, *(1mtr, ch2, skip 1 st) 5 times, 5dc, (ch2, skip 1 st, 1mtr) 4 times, ch2, skip 1 st; rep from * 7 more times, 1mtr, 1dc, ch1.
Row 22 1dc, *(1dc, ch2, skip 1 st) 5 times, 5dc, (ch2, skip 1 st, 1dc) 4 times, ch2, skip 1 st; rep from * 7 more times, 2dc, cc, ch1.
Row 23 1dc, *(ch2, skip 1 st, 1mtr) 5 times, ch2, skip 1 st, 3dc, (ch2, skip 1 st, 1mtr) 5 times; rep from * 7 more times, ch2, skip 1 st, 1dc, ch1.

Row 24 1dc, *(ch2, skip 1 st, 1dc) 5 times, ch2, skip 1 st, 3dc, (ch2, skip 1 st, 1dc) 5 times; rep from * 7 more times, ch2, skip 1 st, 1dc, cc, ch1.

Row 25 1dc, *(1mtr, ch2, skip 1 st) 5 times, 1mtr, 3dc, (1mtr, ch2, skip 1 st) 10 times, 1mtr, 3dc, (1mtr, ch2, skip 1 st) 5 times; rep from * 3 more times, 1mtr, 1dc, ch1.

Row 26 1dc, *(1dc, ch2, skip 1 st) 5 times, 4dc, (1dc, ch2, skip 1 st) 10 times, 4dc, (1dc, ch2, skip 1 st) 5 times; rep from * 3 more times, 2dc, ch1, cc.

Row 27 1dc, *(ch2, skip 1 st, 1mtr) 5 times, 4dc, (ch2, skip 1 st, 1mtr) 5 times, 1dc, (1mtr, ch2, skip 1 st) 5 times, 4dc, (1mtr, ch2, skip 1 st) 4 times, 1mtr; rep from * 3 more times, ch2, skip 1 st, 1dc, ch1.

Row 28 1dc, *(ch2, skip 1 st, 1dc) 5 times, 4dc, (ch2, skip 1 st, 1dc) 5 times, 1dc, (1dc, ch2, skip 1 st) 5 times, 4dc, (1dc, ch2, skip 1 st) 4 times, 1dc; rep from * 3 more times, ch2, skip 1 st, 1dc, cc, ch1.

Row 29 1dc, *(1mtr, ch2, skip 1 st) 4 times, 1mtr, 4dc, (ch2, skip 1 st, 1mtr) 5 times, 3dc, (1mtr, ch2, skip 1 st) 5 times, 4dc, (1mtr, ch2, skip 1 st) 4 times; rep from * 3 more times, 1mtr, 1dc, ch1.

Row 30 1dc, *(1dc, ch2, skip 1 st) 4 times, 5dc, (ch2, skip 1 st, 1dc) 5 times, 3dc, (1dc, ch2, skip 1 st) 5 times, 4dc, (1dc, ch2, skip 1 st) 4 times; rep from * 3 more times, 2dc, cc, ch1.

Row 31 1dc, *(ch2, skip 1 st, 1mtr) 4 times, 5dc, 1mtr, (ch2, skip 1 st, 1mtr) 4 times, 5dc, (1mtr, ch2, skip 1 st) 4 times, 1mtr, 5dc, (1mtr, ch2, skip 1 st) 3 times, 1mtr; rep from * 3 more times, ch2, skip 1 st, 1dc, ch1.

Row 32 1dc, *(ch2, skip 1 st, 1dc) 4 times, 6dc, (ch2, skip 1 st, 1dc) 4 times, 5dc, (1dc, ch2, skip 1 st) 4 times, 6dc, (1dc, ch2, skip 1 st) 3 times, 1dc; rep from * 3 more times, ch2, skip 1 st, 1dc, cc, ch1.

Row 33 1dc, *(1mtr, ch2, skip 1 st) 3 times, 1mtr, 6dc, (ch2, skip 1 st, 1mtr) 4 times, 7dc, (1mtr, ch2, skip 1 st) 4 times, 6dc, (1mtr, ch2, skip 1 st) 3 times; rep from * 3 more times, 1mtr, 1dc, ch1.

Row 34 1dc, *(1dc, ch2, skip 1 st) 3 times, 7dc, (ch2, skip 1 st, 1dc) 4 times, 7dc, (1dc, ch2, skip 1 st) 4 times, 6dc, (1dc, ch2, skip 1 st) 3 times; rep from * 3 more times, 2dc, cc, ch1.

Row 35 1dc, *(ch2, skip 1 st, 1mtr) 3 times, 7dc, 1mtr, (ch2, skip 1 st, 1mtr) 3 times, 9dc, (1mtr, ch2, skip 1 st) 3 times, 1mtr, 7dc, (1mtr, ch2, skip 1 st) 2 times, 1mtr; rep from * 3 more times, ch2, skip 1 st, 1dc, ch1.

Row 36 1dc, *(ch2, skip 1 st, 1dc) 3 times, 8dc, (ch2, skip 1 st, 1dc) 3 times, 9dc, (1dc, ch2, skip 1 st) 3 times, 8dc, (1dc, ch2, skip 1 st) 2 times, 1dc; rep from * 3 more times, ch2, skip 1 st, 1dc, cc, ch1.

Row 37 1dc, *(1mtr, ch2, skip 1 st) twice, 1mtr, 8dc, (ch2, skip 1 st, 1mtr) 3 times, 11dc, (1mtr, ch2, skip 1 st) 3 times, 8dc, (1mtr, ch2, skip 1 st) twice; rep from * 3 more times, 1mtr, 1dc, ch1.

Row 38 1dc, *(1dc, ch2, skip 1 st) twice, 9dc, (ch2, skip 1 st, 1dc) 3 times, 11dc, (1dc, ch2, skip 1 st) 3 times, 8dc, (1dc, ch2, skip 1 st) twice; rep from * 3 more times, 2dc, cc, ch1.

Row 39 1dc, *(ch2, skip 1 st, 1mtr) twice, 9dc, 1mtr, (ch2, skip 1 st, 1mtr) twice, 13dc, (1mtr, ch2, skip 1 st) twice, 1mtr, 9dc, 1mtr, ch2, skip 1 st, 1mtr; rep from * 3 more times, ch2, skip 1 st, 1dc, ch1.

Row 40 1dc, *(ch2, skip 1 st, 1dc) twice, 10dc, (ch2, skip 1 st, 1dc) twice, 13dc, (1dc, ch2, skip 1 st) twice, 11dc, ch2, skip 1 st, 1dc; rep from * 3 more times, ch2, skip 1 st, 1dc, cc, ch1.

Row 41 1dc, *1mtr, ch2, skip 1 st, 1mtr, 10dc, (ch2, skip 1 st, 1mtr) twice, 15dc, (1mtr, ch2, skip 1 st) twice, 10dc, 1mtr, ch2, skip 1 st; rep from * 3 more times, 1mtr, 1dc, ch1.

Row 42 1dc, *1dc, ch2, skip 1 st, 11dc, (ch2, skip 1 st, 1dc) twice, 15dc, (1dc, ch2, skip 1 st) twice, 11dc, ch2, skip 1 st; rep from * 3 more times, 2dc, cc, ch1.

Row 43 1dc, *ch2, skip 1 st, 1mtr, 11dc, 1mtr, ch2, skip 1 st, 1mtr, 17dc, 1mtr, ch2, skip 1 st, 1mtr, 11dc, 1mtr; rep from * 3 more times, ch2, skip 1 st, 1dc, ch1.

Row 44 1dc, *ch2, skip 1 st, 13dc, ch2, skip 1 st, 19dc, ch2, skip 1 st, 13dc; rep from * 3 more times, ch2, skip 1 st, 1dc, cc, ch1.

Row 45 1dc, *1mtr, 13dc, 1mtr, 19dc, 1mtr, 13dc; rep from * 3 more times, 1mtr, 1dc, ch1.

Row 46 1dc in each st to end, cc, ch1.

Row 47 1dc, *ch2, skip 1 st, 13dc, ch2, skip 1 st, 19dc, ch2, skip 1 st, 13dc; rep from * 3 more times, ch2, skip 1 st, 1dc, ch1.

Row 48 1dc, *ch2, skip 1 st, 13dc, ch2, skip 1 st, 19dc, ch2, skip 1 st, 13dc; rep from * 3 more times, ch2, skip 1 st, 1dc, cc, ch1.

Row 49 1dc, *1mtr, ch2, skip 1 st, 11dc, ch2, skip 1 st, 1mtr, ch2, skip 1 st, 17dc, ch2, skip 1 st, 1mtr, ch2, skip 1 st, 11dc, ch2, skip 1 st; rep from * 3 more times, 1mtr, 1dc, ch1.

Row 50 1dc, *1dc, ch2, skip 1 st, 11dc, ch2, skip 1 st, 1dc, ch2, skip 1 st, 17dc, ch2, skip 1 st, 1dc, ch2, skip 1 st, 11dc, ch2, skip 1 st; rep from * 3 more times, 2dc, cc, ch1.

Row 51 1dc, *ch2, skip 1 st, 1mtr, ch2, skip 1 st, 10dc, (1mtr, ch2, skip 1 st) twice, 15dc, (ch2, skip 1 st, 1mtr) twice, 10dc, ch2, skip 1 st, 1mtr; rep from * 3 more times, ch2, skip 1 st, 1dc, ch1.

Row 52 1dc, *ch2, skip 1 st, 1dc, ch2, skip 1 st, 10dc, (1dc, ch2, skip 1 st) twice, 15dc, (ch2, skip 1 st, 1dc) twice, 10dc, ch2, skip 1 st, 1dc; rep from * 3 more times, ch2, skip 1 st, 1dc, cc, ch1.

Row 53 1dc, *(1mtr, ch2, skip 1 st) twice, 9dc, (ch2, skip 1 st, 1mtr) twice, ch2, skip 1 st, 13dc, (ch2, skip 1 st, 1mtr) twice, ch2, skip 1 st, 9dc, ch2, skip 1 st, 1mtr, ch2, skip 1 st; rep from * 3 more times, 1mtr, 1dc, ch1.

Row 54 1dc, *(1dc, ch2, skip 1 st) twice, 9dc, (ch2, skip 1 st, 1dc) twice, ch2, skip 1 st, 13dc, (ch2, skip 1 st, 1dc) twice, ch2, skip 1 st, 9dc, ch2, skip 1 st, 1dc, ch2, skip 1 st; rep from * 3 more times, 2dc, cc, ch1.

Row 55 1dc, *(ch2, skip 1 st, 1mtr) twice, ch2, skip 1 st, 8dc, (1mtr, ch2, skip 1 st) 3 times, 11dc, (ch2, skip 1 st, 1mtr) 3 times, 8dc, (ch2, skip 1 st, 1mtr) twice; rep from * 3 more times, ch2, skip 1 st, 1dc, ch1.

Row 56 1dc, *(ch2, skip 1 st, 1dc) twice, ch2, skip 1 st, 8dc, (1dc, ch2, skip 1 st) 3 times, 11dc, (ch2, skip 1 st, 1dc) 3 times, 8dc, (ch2, skip 1 st, 1dc) twice; rep from * 3 more times, ch2, skip 1 st, 1dc, cc, ch1.

Row 57 1dc, *(1mtr, ch2, skip 1 st) 3 times, 7dc, (ch2, skip 1 st, 1mtr) 3 times, ch2, skip 1 st, 9dc, (ch2, skip 1 st, 1mtr) 3 times, ch2, skip 1 st, 7dc, (ch2, skip 1 st, 1mtr) twice, ch2, skip 1 st; rep from * 3 more times, 1mtr, 1dc, ch1.

Row 58 1dc, *(1dc, ch2, skip 1 st) 3 times, 7dc, (ch2, skip 1 st, 1dc) 3 times, ch2, skip 1 st, 9dc, (ch2, skip 1 st, 1dc) 3 times, ch2, skip 1 st, 7dc, (ch2, skip 1 st, 1dc) twice, ch2, skip 1 st; rep from * 3 more times, 2dc, cc, ch1.

Row 59 1dc, *(ch2, skip 1 st, 1mtr) 3 times, ch2, skip 1 st, 6dc, (1mtr, ch2, skip 1 st) 4 times, 7dc, (ch2, skip 1 st, 1mtr) 4 times, 6dc, (ch2,

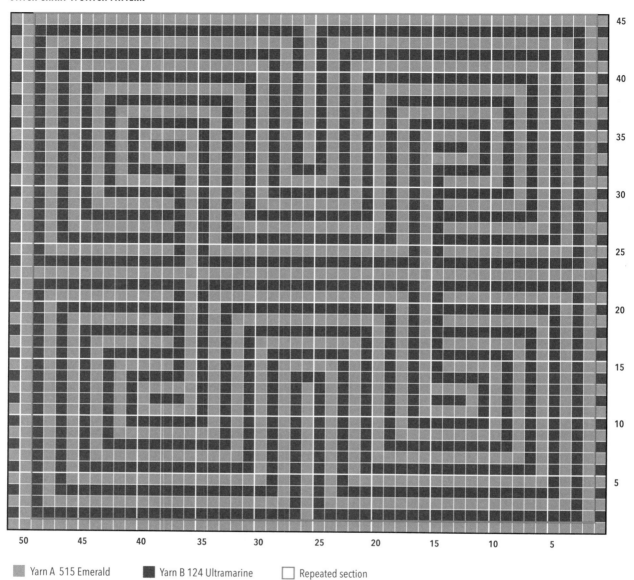

Yarn A 515 Emerald   Yarn B 124 Ultramarine   ☐ Repeated section

skip 1 st, 1mtr) 3 times; rep from * 3 more times, ch2, skip 1 st, 1dc, ch1.

Row 60 1dc, *(ch2, skip 1 st, 1dc) 3 times, ch2, skip 1 st, 6dc, (1dc, ch2, skip 1 st) 4 times, 7dc, (ch2, skip 1 st, 1dc) 4 times, 6dc, (ch2, skip 1 st, 1dc) 3 times; rep from * 3 more times, ch2, skip 1 st, 1dc, cc, ch1.

Row 61 1dc, *(1mtr, ch2, skip 1 st) 4 times, 5dc, (ch2, skip 1 st, 1mtr) 4 times, ch2, skip 1 st, 5dc, (ch2, skip 1 st, 1mtr) 4 times, ch2, skip 1 st, 5dc, (ch2, skip 1 st, 1mtr) 3 times, ch2, skip 1 st; rep from * 3 more times, 1mtr, 1dc, ch1.

Row 62 1dc, *(1dc, ch2, skip 1 st) 4 times, 5dc, (ch2, skip 1 st, 1dc) 4 times, ch2, skip 1 st, 5dc, (ch2, skip 1 st, 1dc) 4 times, ch2, skip 1 st, 5dc, (ch2, skip 1 st, 1dc) 3 times, ch2, skip 1 st; rep from * 3 more times, 2dc, cc, ch1.

Row 63 1dc, *(ch2, skip 1 st, 1mtr) 4 times, ch2, skip 1 st, 4dc, (1mtr, ch2, skip 1 st) 5 times, 3dc, (ch2, skip 1 st, 1mtr) 5 times, 4dc, (ch2, skip 1 st, 1mtr) 4 times; rep from * 3 more times, ch2, skip 1 st, 1dc, ch1.

Row 64 1dc, *(ch2, skip 1 st, 1dc) 4 times, ch2, skip 1 st, 4dc, (1dc, ch2, skip 1 st) 5 times, 3dc, (ch2, skip 1 st, 1dc) 5 times, 4dc, (ch2, skip 1 st, 1dc) 4 times; rep from * 3 more times, ch2, skip 1 st, 1dc, cc, ch1.

Row 65 1dc, *(1mtr, ch2, skip 1 st) 5 times, 4dc, (1mtr, ch2, skip 1 st) 5 times, 1dc, (ch2, skip 1 st, 1mtr) 5 times, 4dc, (ch2, skip 1 st, 1mtr) 4 times, ch2, skip 1 st; rep from * 3 more times, 1mtr, 1dc, ch1.

Row 66 1dc, *(1dc, ch2, skip 1 st) 5 times, 4dc, (1dc, ch2, skip 1 st) 5 times, 1dc, (ch2, skip 1 st, 1dc) 5 times, 4dc, (ch2, skip 1 st, 1dc) 4 times, ch2, skip 1 st; rep from * 3 more times, 2dc, cc, ch1.

Row 67 1dc, *(ch2, skip 1 st, 1mtr) 5 times, ch2, skip 1 st, 3dc, (ch2, skip 1 st, 1mtr) 5 times; rep from * 7 more times, ch2, skip 1 st, 1dc, ch1.

Row 68 1dc, *(ch2, skip 1 st, 1dc) 5 times, ch2, skip 1 st, 3dc, (ch2, skip 1 st, 1dc) 5 times; rep from * 7 more times, ch2, skip 1 st, 1dc, cc, ch1.

Row 69 1dc, *(1mtr, ch2, skip 1 st) 5 times, 1mtr, 3dc, (1mtr, ch2, skip 1 st) 5 times; rep from * 7 more times, 1mtr, 1dc, ch1.

Row 70 1dc, *(1dc, ch2, skip 1 st) 5 times, 4dc, (1dc, ch2, skip 1 st) 5 times; rep from * 7 more times, 2dc, cc, ch1.

Row 71 1dc, *(ch2, skip 1 st, 1mtr) 5 times, 5dc, (1mtr, ch2, skip 1 st) 4 times, 1mtr; rep from * 7 more times, ch2, skip 1 st, 1dc, ch1.

Row 72 1dc, *(ch2, skip 1 st, 1dc) 5 times, 5dc, (1dc, ch2, skip 1 st) 4 times, 1dc; rep from * 7 more times, ch2, skip 1 st, 1dc, cc, ch1.

Row 73 1dc, *(1mtr, ch2, skip 1 st) 4 times, 1mtr, 7dc, (1mtr, ch2, skip 1 st) 4 times; rep from * 7 more times, 1mtr, 1dc, ch1.

Row 74 1dc, *(1dc, ch2, skip 1 st) 4 times, 8dc, (1dc, ch2, skip 1 st) 4 times; rep from * 7 more times, 2dc, cc, ch1.

Row 75 1dc, *(ch2, skip 1 st, 1mtr) 4 times, 9dc, (1mtr, ch2, skip 1 st) 3 times, 1mtr; rep from * 7 more times, ch2, skip 1 st, 1dc, ch1.

Row 76 1dc, *(ch2, skip 1 st, 1dc) 4 times, 9dc, (1dc, ch2, skip 1 st) 3 times, 1dc; rep from * 7 more times, ch2, skip 1 st, 1dc, cc, ch1.

Row 77 1dc, *(1mtr, ch2, skip 1 st) 3 times, 1mtr, 11dc, (1mtr, ch2, skip 1 st) 3 times; rep from * 7 more times, 1mtr, 1dc, ch1.

Row 78 1dc, *(1dc, ch2, skip 1 st) 3 times, 12dc, (1dc, ch2, skip 1 st) 3 times; rep from * 7 more times, 2dc, cc, ch1.

Row 79 1dc, *(ch2, skip 1 st, 1mtr) 3 times, 13dc, (1mtr, ch2, skip 1 st)

twice, 1mtr; rep from * 7 more times, ch2, skip 1 st, 1dc, ch1.

Row 80 1dc, *(ch2, skip 1 st, 1dc) 3 times, 13dc, (1dc, ch2, skip 1 st) twice, 1dc; rep from * 7 more times, ch2, skip 1 st, 1dc, cc, ch1.

Row 81 1dc, *(1mtr, ch2, skip 1 st) twice, 1mtr, 15dc, (1mtr, ch2, skip 1 st) twice; rep from * 7 more times, 1mtr, 1dc, ch1.

Row 82 1dc, *(1dc, ch2, skip 1 st) twice, 16dc, (1dc, ch2, skip 1 st) twice; rep from * 7 more times, 2dc, cc, ch1.

Row 83 1dc, *(ch2, skip 1 st, 1mtr) twice, 17dc, 1mtr, ch2, skip 1 st, 1mtr; rep from * 7 more times, ch2, skip 1 st, 1dc, ch1.

Row 84 1dc, *(ch2, skip 1 st, 1dc) twice, 17dc, 1dc, ch2, skip 1 st, 1dc; rep from * 7 more times, ch2, skip 1 st, 1dc, cc, ch1.

Row 85 1dc, *1mtr, ch2, skip 1 st, 1mtr, 19dc, 1mtr, ch2, skip 1 st; rep from * 7 more times, 1mtr, 1dc, ch1.

Row 86 1dc, *1dc, ch2, skip 1 st, 21dc, ch2, skip 1 st; rep from * 7 more times, 2dc, cc, ch1.

Row 87 1dc, *ch2, skip 1 st, 1mtr, 21dc, 1mtr; rep from * 7 more times, ch2, skip 1 st, 1dc, ch1.

Row 88 1dc, *ch2, skip 1 st, 23dc; rep from * 7 more times, ch2, skip 1 st, 1dc, cc, ch1.

Row 89 1dc, *1mtr, 23dc; rep from * 7 more times, 1mtr, 1dc, ch1.

Row 90 1dc in each st to end, cc, ch1.

Rows 91-354 Rep Rows 3-90 a further 3 times. Fasten off Yarn B at end of Row 352. Keep Yarn A attached at end of Row 354 for Border.

BORDER

Note: Work around blanket with Yarn A and RS facing. When you reach cnr after 195 dc, rotate blanket 90 degrees and work along longer side. Every row end counts as 1 st.

Round 1 (RS) Ch1, 195dc, ch2, 2dc, (skip 1 st, 5dc) 58 times, skip 1 st, 3dc, ch2, 195dc, ch2, 2dc, (skip 1 st, 5dc) 58 times, skip 1 st, 3dc, ch2, ss to first dc to join. [980 dc, 4 ch-2 sps]

Round 2 Ch1, 1dc in first st, 194dc, (1dc, ch2, 1dc) in ch-2 sp, 295dc, (1dc, ch2, 1dc) in ch-2 sp, 195dc, (1dc, ch2, 1dc) in ch-2 sp, 295dc, (1dc, ch2, 1dc) in ch-2 sp, ss to first dc. [988 dc, 4 ch-2 sps]

Round 3 Ch1, 1dc in first st, 196dc, (1dc, ch2, 1dc) in ch-2 sp, 297dc, (1dc, ch2, 1dc) in ch-2 sp, 197dc, (1dc, ch2, 1dc) in ch-2 sp, 297dc, (1dc, ch2, 1dc) in ch-2 sp, ss to first dc to join, fasten off Yarn A. [996 dc, 4 ch-2 sps]

TO FINISH

Weave in all ends and block to measurements.

NISHIO SWEATER

By Susan Walsh

peppergoose.design

MEASUREMENTS

See Measurements Table

ABBREVIATIONS

See back cover flap*

MATERIALS

Scheepjes Our Tribe (70% Merino Superwash, 30% Polyamide; 100g/420m)

977 A Spoonful of Yarn x 5 (5: 6: 7: 8) balls, plus 1 ball for swatching (see Pattern Notes)

5mm crochet hook

4mm crochet hook

Stitch markers

GAUGE/TENSION

Main fabric: 16 sts and 18 rows to measure 10 x 10cm over alternating rows of dc flo and htr using a 5mm hook after blocking.

SPECIAL ABBREVIATIONS

ext ch extension chain: ch(s) worked at end of a row to form a base for next row

fdc foundation double crochet: insert hook in base of prev st, yoh, draw through (2 lps on hook), yoh, draw through first lp for base of next fdc (2 lps on hook), yoh, draw through both lps on hook

feature ss seam with WS tog, 1ss in inner lps of each aligned st to end

flat ss seam with RS tog, 1ss in outer lps of each aligned st to end

Note: If ss seams are too tight despite trying a bigger hook, ch1 between each ss to allow finished seam to flex and move with main fabric.

JAYG Join As You Go

PATTERN NOTES

Back Piece, Front Piece and Sleeves are made separately, all in vertically oriented rows, working armhole to armhole, starting at left side. Bodice is assembled by hand sewn side seams through aligned stitches. Ensure all sewn and crocheted seams can still stretch and move with main fabric. Each lower sleeve is edged, slip stitch seamed into a tube shape, then cuff is finished with JAYG Dc Ribbing. Each Raglan join is made by edging bodice side, then sleeve side, then slip stitch seamed together. After second raglan join is made, Neckline is finished with shorter JAYG Dc Ribbing. Finally, hem is finished with JAYG Dc Ribbing.

Sleeves and Bodice increase in length quite significantly during wet blocking to size indicated in Schematic 1. Follow blocking instructions to finish garment.

0.25cm seam allowance for sewn side seams and 0.5cm allowance for dc edging are included in measurements.

Before starting garment, swatch in main patt fabric 28 rows x 26 sts wide, starting with foundation row of 26fdc to check gauge and understand ribbed main fabric. See Back Left Side to Armhole shaping for extra clarity on technique.

INSTRUCTIONS

BACK

Left Side

With 5mm hook, ch2, 1fdc in second ch from hook, 52 (51: 52: 54: 55) fdc, turn. [53 (52: 53: 55: 56) fdc]

Row 1 (RS) Ch1 (does not count as st throughout), 1htr in each dc to end, turn. [53 (52: 53: 55: 56) htr]

Row 2 (WS) Ch1, 1dc flo (work into lowest front lp throughout) in each htr to end, turn. [53 (52: 53: 55: 56) dc flo] *Note: For last st of this row, lowest front lp can be hard to find. If necessary, tease it out with a smaller hook or needle, then work into it. Check you have a raised "ch" shape on RS.*

Last two rows form main fabric patt.

Cont in main fabric patt as set for 1 (3: 3: 5: 5) more rows, ending with a RS row, at end of last row cont with 3 ext ch, turn.

Armhole Shaping

Row 1 (WS) Ch1, 1dc (worked into horizontal bar at back of ch) in each of next 3 ext ch, 1dc flo in each htr to end, turn. [56 (55: 56: 58: 59)sts]

Row 2 (RS) Ch1, 1htr in each dc to end, cont with 3 ext ch, turn. [59 (58: 59: 61: 62) sts]

Last two rows form armhole inc patt.

Cont in armhole inc patt as set for 22 (24: 26: 26: 28) more rows, ending with a RS row, turn. [92 (94: 98: 100: 104) sts, including 3 ext ch at end of last row]

Measurements Table

Size	S	M	L	XL	XXL
To fit Bust (cm)	86-91.5	96.5-101.5	106.5-111.5	116.5-122	127-132
To fit Bust (in)	34-36	38-40	42-44	46-48	50-52
Actual Bust (cm)	96	105	114	122.5	131.5
Actual Bust (in)	38	41.5	45	48	52
Actual Length (cm)	69.8	71	74	75	77.5
Actual Length (in)	27.5	28	29	29.5	30.5

SCHEMATIC 1:
GARMENT MEASUREMENTS

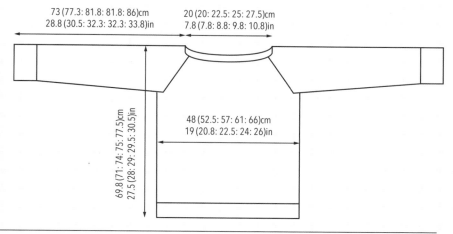

73 (77.3: 81.8: 81.8: 86)cm
28.8 (30.5: 32.3: 32.3: 33.8)in

20 (20: 22.5: 25: 27.5)cm
7.8 (7.8: 8.8: 9.8: 10.8)in

69.8 (71: 74: 75: 77.5)cm
27.5 (28: 29: 29.5: 30.5)in

48 (52.5: 57: 61: 66)cm
19 (20.8: 22.5: 24: 26)in

BACK NECK

Row 1 (WS) Ch1, 1dc in next ch, dc2tog flo over next 2 ch, 1dc flo in each htr to end, turn. [91 (93: 97: 99: 103) dc flo]

Row 2 (RS) Ch1, 1htr in each dc to end, turn. [91 (93: 97: 99: 103) htr]

Row 3 Ch1, 1dc flo, dc2tog flo, 1dc flo in each rem htr to end, turn. [90 (92: 96: 98: 102) dc flo]

Last two rows form neck dec patt. **

Cont in neck dec patt as set for 0 (0: 2: 2: 4) more rows, ending with a WS row, turn. [90 (92: 95: 97: 100) dc flo]

Cont in main fabric patt without shaping for 27 (27: 27: 31: 31) more rows, ending with a RS row, turn.

Next row (WS) Ch1, 1dc flo, 2dc in next htr, 1dc flo in each rem htr to end, turn. [91 (93: 96: 98: 101) dc flo]

Next row (RS) Ch1, 1htr in each dc to end, turn. [91 (93: 96: 98: 101) htr]

Last two rows form neck inc patt.

Cont in neck inc patt as set for 1 (1: 3: 3: 5) more rows, ending with a WS row, turn. [92 (94: 98: 100: 104) dc flo] ***

Armhole Shaping

Row 1 (RS) Ch1, 1htr in each dc along to last 3 dc, leave last 3 dc unworked, turn. [89 (91: 95: 97: 101) htr]

Row 2 (WS) 1dc flo in each htr to end, turn. [89 (91: 95: 97: 101) dc flo]

Last two rows form armhole dec patt.

Cont in armhole dec patt for 23 (25: 27: 27: 29) more rows, ending with a RS row, turn. [53 (52: 53: 55: 56) htr]

Right Side

Cont in main fabric patt for 2 (4: 4: 6: 6) more rows, ending with a RS row.

Fasten off.

FRONT

Work as for back to **.

Cont in neck dec patt as set for 6 (6: 8: 8: 10) more rows, ending with a WS row, turn. [87 (89: 92: 94: 97) dc flo]

Cont straight in main fabric patt for 15 (15: 15: 19: 19) more rows, ending with a RS row, turn.

Next row (WS) Ch1, 1dc flo in next htr, 2dc flo, 1dc flo in each rem htr to end, turn. [88 (90: 93: 95: 98) dc flo]

Next row (RS) Ch1, 1htr in each dc to end, turn. [88 (90: 93: 95: 98) htr]

Cont in neck inc patt as set for 7 (7: 9: 9: 11) more rows, ending with a WS row, turn. [92 (94: 98: 100: 104) dc flo]

Work as for back from *** to end.

SLEEVE (MAKE 2)

With 5mm hook, ch2, 1fdc in second ch from hook, 4 (3: 7: 7: 5)fdc, turn. [5 (4: 8: 8: 6) fdc]

Row 1 (RS) Ch1, 1htr in each st to end, turn. [5 (4: 8: 8: 6) htr]

Row 2 (WS) Ch1, 1dc flo in each htr to end, cont with 11 (10: 10: 10: 11) ext ch, turn. [5 (4: 8: 8: 6) dc flo, 11 (10: 10: 10: 11) ch]

Last two rows form sleeve inc patt.

Cont in sleeve inc patt for 1 (3: 3: 5: 5) more rows, (working htr into horizontal bar at back of ext ch), ending with a RS row, cont with 3 ext ch at end of last row, turn. [19 (27: 31: 41: 42) sts, including 3 ext ch at end of last row]

Armhole Shaping

Starting with a WS row, cont in both armhole inc patt as for back at neck end, AND sleeve inc patt at cuff end for 7 (7: 7: 5: 5) rows, ending with a WS row, turn. [72 (76: 80: 77: 81) sts]

Cont in both armhole inc patt at neck end, AND main fabric patt at cuff end for 17 (19: 21: 23: 25) more rows, ending with a RS row, turn. [99 (106: 113: 113: 120) sts, including 3 ext ch at end of last row]

Cont in main fabric patt for 9 (9: 11: 11: 11) more rows, ending with a WS row, turn. [99 (106: 113: 113: 120) sts]

Cont in both armhole dec patt as for back at neck end, AND main fabric patt at cuff end for 17 (19: 21: 23: 25) rows, ending with a RS row, turn. [72 (76: 80: 77: 81) sts]

Note: For sleeve dec patt (begins next row), simply leave last 11 (10: 10: 10: 11) htr unworked at end of each WS row, turn.

Cont in armhole dec patt at neck end, AND sleeve dec patt *(see Note above)* at cuff end for 8 (8: 8: 6: 6) more rows, ending with a RS row, turn. [16 (24: 28: 38: 39) htr]

Cont in sleeve dec patt at cuff end, AND main fabric patt at armhole end for 2 (4: 4: 6: 6) rows, ending with a RS row. [5 (4: 8: 8: 6) dc flo]

Fasten off.

STITCH CHART 1: EDGING OF SLEEVE IN PREPARATION FOR SEAM

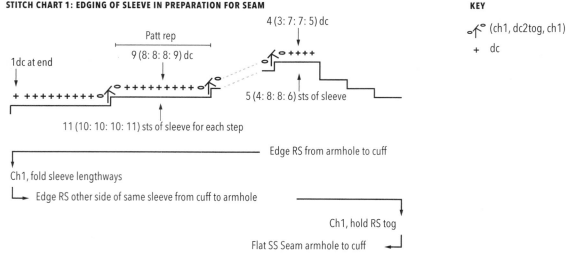

KEY

○↑° (ch1, dc2tog, ch1)

+   dc

STITCH CHART 2: JAYG DC RIBBING

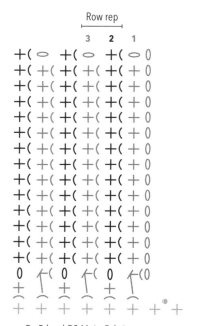

Dc Edged RS Main Fabric
of Sleeve or Hem

KEY

○   ch

+   dc

⊥   dc blo

↑⟨   dc2tog blo

•   ss join to close round of
dc edging of main fabric

STITCH CHART 3: RAGLAN EDGING

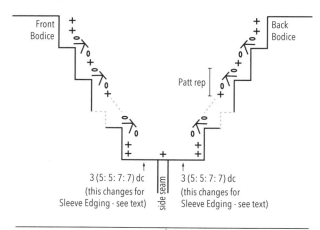

ASSEMBLY

Sew side seams through aligned sts to match raised ch effect on main fabric. *Note: This effectively adds two rows to total circumference of bodice for edging purposes at bottom hem (see Hem Edging below).* For Left Side Seam, lay RS of both Back and Front Pieces facing up on a table to align chs at base of each fdc of Back Piece with tops of htr sts of Front Piece. Note that 'lowest front lp' of last htr row of Front Piece *(which has been used to dc into for main fabric pattern)* is lying on WS. Thread tapestry needle with approx. 1.2m yarn, start at armhole end, insert needle WS to RS up through lowest front lp of last htr of last row of Front Piece, but do not pull all the way through *(leave approx. 15cm tail)*. Insert needle RS to WS down under the 2 lps of ch at base of beg fdc of Back Piece. Cont to sew WS to RS up through lowest front lp of Front Piece, then RS to WS down through the 2 ch lps at base of corresponding fdc of Back Piece for each sequentially aligned st pair, ensuring sewing tension matches drape of fabric. Check tension every 6-8 sts. This is essential as bodice will lengthen when blocked. Once seam is complete, leave starting and finishing tails to hide in future edging.
Rep for Right Side Seam.

SLEEVES (ASSEMBLE BOTH IN SAME WAY)

(See Stitch Chart 1: Edging of Sleeve in Preparation for Seam)

Sleeve Edging

With 5mm hook and RS facing, starting at armhole end of sleeve, working towards cuff, 1dc in each of first 4 (3: 7: 7: 5) sts, (ch1, dc2tog over next 2 sts over the step down in fabric *(i.e. last unworked st at top side of step and first unworked st at low side of step)*, ch1, 1dc in each of next 9 (8: 8: 8: 9) sts) a total of 5 (6: 6: 6: 6) times, 1dc in last st at cuff, [65 (70: 74: 74: 78) sts], ch1 (does not count as st), fold sleeve in half lengthwise to work RS from other end of cuff up other side of sleeve to armhole, 1dc in each of first 10 (9: 9: 9: 10) sts, (ch1, dc2tog over next 2 sts over the step up in fabric *(again, last and first unworked sts)*, ch1, 1dc in each of next 9 (8: 8: 8: 9) sts) a total of 5 (6: 6: 6: 6) times, 1dc in each of last 4 (3: 7: 7: 5) sts. [65 (70: 74: 74: 78) sts]

Seam

Ch1 (does not count as st), work flat ss seam with RS tog, from armhole to cuff. [65 (70: 74: 74: 78) sts] *Note: Sleeve is now an inside-out tube.*

Cuff Edging

Ch1 to change direction (does not count as st), change to 4mm hook, edge RS of cuff by working 1dc in each row end and 3dc in ss seam (1 in each edging row, 1 in end of seam) around, 1ss to beg dc to join. [46 (50: 56: 60: 64) dc]

JAYG Dc Ribbing

(See Stitch Chart 2: JAYG Dc Ribbing)

Ch15, turn.

Row 1 (RS) Ch1 (counts as 1 dc), 1dc in third ch from hook and in each of next 12 ch, dc2tog blo over last ch and next dc along garment edge, 1dc blo in next dc along garment edge, turn. [14 dc, 1 dc2tog blo, 1 dc blo]

Row 2 (WS) Ch1 (counts as 1 dc), 1dc blo in fourth st from hook and in each rem 13 dc across, turn. [15 dc blo]

Row 3 Ch1 (counts as 1 dc), 1dc blo in third st from hook and in each of next 12 dc, dc2tog blo over last dc and next dc along garment edge, 1dc blo in next dc along garment edge, turn. [14 dc blo, 1 dc2tog blo, 1 dc blo]

Rep Rows 2-3 around to end of Row 44 (48: 54: 58: 62) of Dc Ribbing, with WS tog, 1ss in aligned blo of front fabric and unworked lp of ribbing foundation ch of back fabric across to close ribbing. [15 ss] Fasten off.

LEFT RAGLAN EDGES

Raglan Edging

(See Stitch Chart 3: Raglan Edging)

With 4mm hook and RS facing, starting at neckline end of back left bodice raglan, working towards Left armhole, 1dc in each of first 2 sts, (ch1, dc2tog over next 2 sts over the step down in fabric, ch1, 1dc in next st) a total of 12 (13: 14: 14: 15) times, 1dc in next st, (armhole incs now edged), cont with 3 (5: 5: 7: 7)dc across side rows (i.e. 1dc per row end), 1dc over side seam, 3 (5: 5: 7: 7)dc across side rows, cont up front left armhole incs with 1dc in each of first 2 sts, (ch1, dc2tog over next 2 sts over the step up in fabric, ch1, 1dc in next st) a total of 12 (13: 14: 14: 15) times, 1dc in last st. [109 (121: 129: 133: 141) dc]

Ch1 (does not count as st), cont with rep Raglan Edging technique along RS of a sleeve raglan (now designated left sleeve), starting at front neckline end, working down to armhole and finishing at back neckline end, including 2 dc2tog across side rows (one on each side of the dc in sleeve seam) so edging st counts match. [109 (121: 129: 133: 141) dc]

Seam

Ch1 (does not count as st), work feature ss seam with WS tog, from back neckline to front neckline. [109 (121: 129: 133: 141) ss] Fasten off.

RIGHT RAGLAN EDGES

Rep edging and seaming technique as for left raglan edges, but do not fasten off.

NECKLINE EDGING

Ch1 to change direction (counts as 1 dc), then edge RS circumference of neckline by working 1dc per row end *(include ext ch at beg of each neckline of each piece as a row)* and 2dc per ss seam around, 1ss to beg dc to join. [96 (96: 108: 116: 124) dc]

Neckline JAYG Dc Ribbing

Work as JAYG Dc Ribbing technique for sleeve cuff, but with 9 fewer sts for all ribbing rows around Neckline, so start with ch6.

Work 94 (94: 106: 114: 122) rows. With WS tog, 1ss in aligned blo of front fabric and unworked lp of ribbing foundation ch of back fabric across to close ribbing. [6 ss] Fasten off.

HEMLINE

Hem Edging

With 4mm hook and RS facing, work 1dc per row end and 1dc per ss seam around, 1ss to beg dc to join. [176 (192: 208: 224: 140) dc]

JAYG Dc Ribbing

Work as JAYG Dc Ribbing for sleeve cuff to end of Row 174 (190: 206: 222: 138) of Dc Ribbing. With WS tog, 1ss in aligned blo of front fabric and unworked lp of ribbing foundation ch of back fabric across to close ribbing. [15 ss] Fasten off.

TO FINISH

Weave in all ends, wet block to measurements, lay flat to dry, do not stretch fabric while wet. *Note: The variable thickness of yarn pulls in more over thinner sections of Dc Ribbing across hem (less so on cuffs) during wet blocking, so height of bodice will vary once dry.* Once dry, gently steam block as required: pin a section (with glass-headed pins) on lower edge of hem ribbing to Schematic measurements, gently stroke bodice fabric away from ribbing to create desired look. With iron on wool setting, hover iron 1-2cm over fabric, holding in place for approx. 5 seconds, fan fabric thoroughly to cool, move pins and rep for next section. Insert tightly rolled towel into each sleeve, steam for 2 seconds per section. Avoid steaming cuffs to maintain elasticity.

GINGER ROOT GLOVES
By Margje Enting

MEASUREMENTS
21cm (8.3in) circumference
x 18.5cm (7.3in) long

ABBREVIATIONS
See back cover flap

MATERIALS
Scheepjes Metropolis (75% Merino Extra Fine, 25% Nylon; 50g/200m)
Yarn A: 035 Seoul x 1 ball
Yarn B: 030 Toulouse x 1 ball
Yarn C: 033 Atlanta x 1 ball
Yarn D: 066 Copenhagen x 1 ball
Yarn E: 065 Liverpool x 1 ball
Scrap yarn in contrast colour (2 x 50cm lengths)
Set of 2.5mm dpn's
Stitch marker

GAUGE/TENSION
30 sts and 36 rounds to measure 10 x 10cm in Fair Isle knitting using 2.5mm needles.

PATTERN NOTES
The pattern is worked in the Fair Isle (stranded) style. Knit a left hand and a right hand glove.

INSTRUCTIONS

With Yarn A, cast on 64 sts. Join to work in the round, taking care not to twist sts, PM to mark beg of round.
Work Rounds 1-42 from Main Chart twice across each round. Work each square in colour given on chart, knitting plain squares and purling squares with a line through them.

For row 43, left hand thumb position is marked on Main Chart with a black line, and right hand thumb position is marked with a blue line.
Thumb row 43 (left hand) K18 in patt, mark location of thumb with contrast colour yarn as folls: k12 for thumb with scrap yarn (tie loose ends of scrap yarn tog so that it does not pull out), slide thumb sts back onto left needle and k them again in patt, cont in patt to end of round.
Thumb row 43 (right hand) K2 in patt, mark location of thumb with contrast colour yarn as folls: k12 for thumb with scrap yarn (tie loose ends of scrap yarn tog so that it does not pull out), slide thumb sts back onto left needle and k them again in patt, cont in patt to end of round.
Cont to work Rounds 44-75 from Main Chart as set.
Cast off with Yarn A.
Thumb
Pick up 12 sts directly above scrap yarn (pick up right leg of each st and work from right to left). Take a second needle and pick up sts directly below scrap yarn in same way. Remove scrap yarn. Whilst working Round 1, spread sts over 3 dpn's.
Round 1 With Yarn A, k12 from first needle, pick up 2 sts, k12 from second needle, pick up 2 sts. [28 sts]
Work Rounds 1-13 from Thumb Chart.

TO FINISH
Weave in all ends.

THUMB CHART

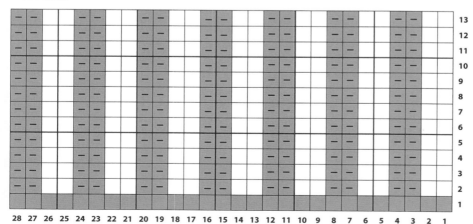

Yarn A 035 Seoul

Yarn A purl 035 Seoul

MAIN CHART

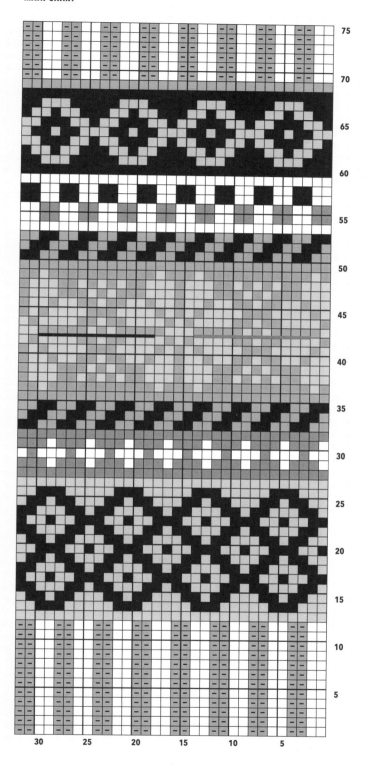

Yarn A 035 Seoul

Yarn A purl 035 Seoul

Yarn B 030 Toulouse

Yarn C 033 Atlanta

Yarn D 066 Copenhagen

Yarn E 065 Liverpool

Left hand thumb position

Right hand thumb position

SPICE MARKET SNOOD
By Nerissa Muijs
missneriss.com

MEASUREMENTS
100cm (39.5in) circumference
x 50cm (19.8in) height
after blocking

ABBREVIATIONS
See back cover flap

MATERIALS
Scheepjes Namaste (50% Virgin Wool, 50% Acrylic; 100g/85m)
604 Locust x 7 balls or 618 Gate x 7 balls
10mm crochet hook

GAUGE/TENSION
10 sts and 8 rounds to measure 10 x 10cm over patt using 10mm hook before blocking.

SPECIAL ABBREVIATIONS
5ttr-cl 5 triple treble crochet cluster stitch: *yoh 3 times, insert hook in st, pull up lp, (yoh, draw through 2 lps) 3 times; rep from * 4 more times in same st, yoh, draw through all 6 lps
fhtr foundation half treble crochet: ch3, yoh, insert hook in third ch from hook, yoh, pull up lp (3 lps on hook), yoh, draw through 1 lp (1 ch made), yoh, draw through 3 lps (1 htr made), *yoh, insert hook in last ch made, pull up lp (3 lps on hook), yoh, draw through 1 lp (1 ch made), yoh, draw through 3 lps (1 htr made); rep from * for each fhtr

PATTERN NOTES
5ttr-cl sts are *always* worked into an unworked st 3 rounds below. When working cluster rounds, 'skip 1 htr' means working into the same st 3 rounds below and leaving that same st in the active round unworked. The snood is worked bottom up with some shaping in later rounds for a slightly more fitted look.

INSTRUCTIONS

Round 1 Leaving a 15cm tail, work 80fhtr, ss to first fhtr to join, being sure not to twist foundation ch. Weave tail through bottom of first and last sts to close ch.
Round 2 Ch2 (does not count as st throughout), 1htr in same st, 2htr, ch1, skip 1 htr, *3htr, ch1, skip 1 htr; rep from * to end, ss to first htr. [80 sts]
Round 3 Ch2, 1htr in same st, 1htr in each htr and ch-sp to end, ss to first htr.
Round 4 Ch2, 1htr in same st, 1htr in each htr to end, ss to first htr.
Round 5 Ch2, 1htr in same st, 2htr, 5ttr-cl in unworked st 3 rounds below, skip 1 htr, *3htr, 5ttr-cl in unworked st 3 rounds below, skip 1 htr; rep from * to end, ss to first htr.
Round 6 Ch2, 1htr in same st, 1htr, ch1, skip 1 htr, *3htr, ch1, skip 1 htr; rep from * to last st, 1htr, ss to first htr.
Round 7 Rep Round 3.
Round 8 Rep Round 4.
Round 9 Ch2, 1htr in same st, 1htr, 5ttr-cl in unworked st 3 rounds below, skip 1 htr, *3htr, 5ttr-cl in unworked st 3 rounds below, skip 1 htr; rep from * to last st, 1htr, ss to first htr.

Round 10 Ch2, 1htr in same st, ch1, skip 1 htr, *3htr, ch1, skip 1 htr; rep from * to last 2 sts, 2htr, ss to first htr.
Round 11 Rep Round 3.
Round 12 Rep Round 4.
Round 13 Ch2, 1htr in same st, 5ttr-cl in unworked st 3 rounds below, skip 1 htr, *3htr, 5ttr-cl in unworked st 3 rounds below, skip 1 htr; rep from * to last 2 sts, 2htr, ss to first htr.
Round 14 Ss in next st (big lp of the cluster), ch2, 1htr in same st, 2htr, ch1, skip 1 htr, *3htr, ch1, skip 1 htr; rep from * to last 3 sts, 3htr, ch1, skip first htr of prev round, ss to first htr in this round (new start of round position).
Rounds 15-21 Rep Rounds 3-9.
Round 22 Ch2, htr2tog over first two sts, 3htr, ch1, skip 1 htr, *3htr, ch1, skip 1 htr; rep from * to last 2 sts, 2htr, ss to first htr2tog. [79 sts]
Round 23 Ch2, htr2tog over first two sts, 1htr in each htr and ch-sp to end, ss to first htr2tog. [78 sts]
Round 24 Ch2, htr2tog over first two sts, 1htr in each st to end, ss to first htr2tog. [77 sts]
Round 25 Ch2, htr2tog over first two sts, 5ttr-cl in unworked st 3 rounds below, skip 1 htr, *3htr, 5ttr-cl in unworked st 3 rounds below, skip 1 htr; rep from * to last 2 sts, 2htr, ss to first htr2tog. [76 sts]
Round 26 Rep Round 14 (new start of round position).
Round 27 Rep Round 3.
Round 28 Rep Round 4.
Round 29 Rep Round 5.
Round 30 Ch2, htr2tog over first two sts, 4htr, ch1, skip 1 htr, *3htr, ch1, skip 1 htr; rep from * to last 3 sts, 3htr, ss to first htr2tog. [75 sts]
Round 31 Rep Round 23. [74 sts]
Round 32 Rep Round 24. [73 sts]
Round 33 Ch2, htr2tog over first two sts, 1htr, 5ttr-cl in unworked st 3 rounds below, skip 1 htr, *3htr, 5ttr-cl in unworked st 3 rounds below, skip 1 htr; rep from * to last 3 sts, 3htr, ss to first htr2tog. [72 sts]
Round 34 Ch2, 1htr in same st, ch1, skip 1 htr, *3htr, ch1, skip 1 htr; rep from * to last 4 sts, 4htr, ss to first htr.
Round 35 Rep Round 3.
Round 36 Rep Round 4.
Round 37 Ch2, 1htr in same st, 5ttr-cl in unworked st 3 rounds below, skip 1 htr, *3htr, 5ttr-cl in unworked st 3 rounds below, skip 1 htr; rep from * to last 4 sts, 4htr, ss to first htr.
Round 38 Ch2, htr2tog over first two sts, 1htr in each st to end, ss to first htr2tog. [71 sts]
Round 39 Ch2, 1htr in each st to end, ss to first htr. Fasten off.
Turn work upside down, join yarn to any foundation ch.
Next round Ch2, 1htr in each ch to end, ss to first htr.

TO FINISH
Fasten off, weave in ends, block to measurements.

HONEY PONCHO
By Tatsiana Kupryianchyk
lillabjorncrochet.com

MATERIALS
Scheepjes Merino Soft Brush (50% Wool Superwash Merino, 25% Microfibre, 25% Acrylic; 50g/105m)
251 Avercamp x 17 (21) balls
5mm crochet hook
5.5mm crochet hook
2 x Button Flower, no. 5623-40-932
4 stitch markers

GAUGE/TENSION
20 sts and 10 rows to measure 10 x 10cm over (1tr, ch1) using a 5mm hook after blocking.

SPECIAL ABBREVIATIONS
pc popcorn: work 5tr in same st, drop lp from hook, insert hook from front to back through top of first tr made, place dropped lp on hook, yoh and draw through st

PATTERN NOTES
Honey Poncho was designed with approx. 70-80cm of positive ease. The poncho consists of one back and two front panels sewn together on shoulders. The hem, side edges and collar are added at the end.

INSTRUCTIONS

FRONT LEFT PANEL
Row 1 (WS) With 5mm hook, ch74 (98), 1tr in sixth ch from hook, *ch3, skip 2 ch, 1dc in next ch, ch3, skip 2 ch, 1tr in next ch; rep from * to last 2 ch, ch1, skip 1 ch, 1tr in last ch, turn. [14 (18) tr, 11 (15) dc, 22 (30) ch-3 sps, 2 ch-1 sps]
Row 2 (RS) Ch4 (counts as 1 tr and ch-1 sp throughout), skip ch-1 sp, 1tr in next tr, *(ch1, 1tr in next ch-3 sp) twice, ch1, 1tr in next tr; rep from * to last ch-1 sp, ch1, 1tr in top of beg 3-ch, turn. [36 (48) tr, 35 (47) ch-1 sps]
Row 3 Ch4, skip ch-1 sp, 1tr in next tr, *ch3, skip next ch-1 sp and tr, 1dc in next ch-1 sp, ch3, skip next tr and ch-1 sp, 1tr in next tr; rep from * to last ch-1 sp, ch1, 1tr in top of beg 3-ch, turn. [14 (18) tr, 11 (15) dc, 22 (30) ch-3 sps, 2 ch-1 sps]

Measurements Table

Size	XS-M	L-XXL
Width across back (cm)	96	120
Width across back (in)	37.8	47.3
Length (cm)	83	83
Length (in)	32.8	32.8

SCHEMATIC 1: GARMENT MEASUREMENTS

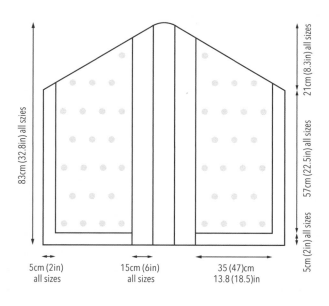

83cm (32.8in) all sizes

21cm (8.3in) all sizes

57cm (22.5in) all sizes

5cm (2in) all sizes

5cm (2in) all sizes

15cm (6in) all sizes

35 (47)cm 13.8 (18.5)in

Row 4 Ch4, skip ch-1 sp, 1tr in next tr, *(ch1, 1tr in next ch-3 sp) twice, ch1, 1tr in next tr, (ch1, 1tr in next ch-3 sp) twice, ch1, pc in next tr; rep from * to last 2 ch-3 sps, (ch1, 1tr in next ch-3 sp) twice, ch1, 1tr in next tr, ch1, 1tr in top of beg 3-ch, turn. [31 (41) tr, 5 (7) pc, 35 (47) ch-1 sps]
Row 5 Rep Row 3.
Row 6 Rep Row 2.
Row 7 Rep Row 3.
Row 8 Ch4, skip ch-1 sp, 1tr in next tr, (ch1, 1tr in next ch-3 sp) twice, ch1, pc in next tr, *(ch1, 1tr in next ch-3 sp) twice, ch1, 1tr in next tr, (ch1, 1tr in next ch-3 sp) twice, ch1, pc in next tr; rep from * to last ch-1 sp, replacing last pc with 1tr, ch1, 1tr in top of beg 3-ch, turn. [31 (41) tr, 5 (7) pc, 35 (47) ch-1 sps]
Row 9 Rep Row 3.
Row 10 Rep Row 2.
Row 11 Rep Row 3.
Rows 12-51 Rep Rows 4-11 five more times.
Rows 52-57 Rep Rows 4-9 once.
Shape Shoulder
Rows 58-78 Follow either written instructions below or Stitch Chart 1 for shaping shoulder. *Note: Chart shows Size XS-M. Size L-XXL will have more sts left after Row 78.*

STITCH CHART 1: SHAPING SHOULDERS ON FRONT LEFT PANEL

Chart shows Size XS-M

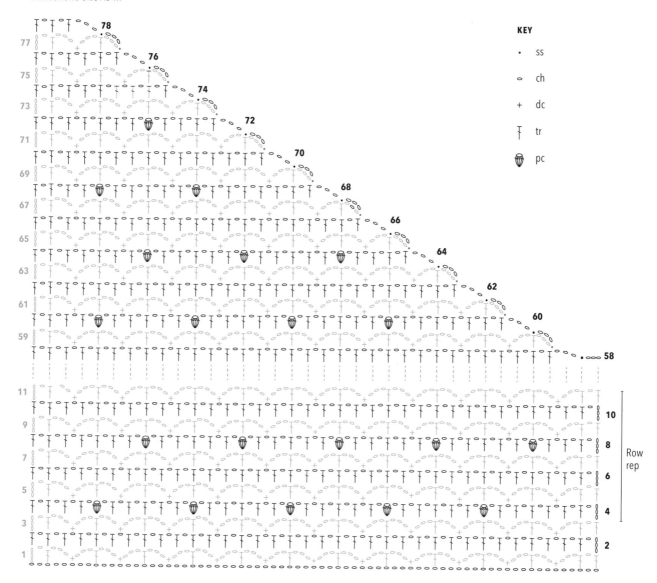

KEY

• ss

o ch

+ dc

T tr

pc

Row 58 Ch3, skip ch-1 sp, ss in next tr, ch3, skip next ch-3 sp and dc, 1tr in next ch-3 sp, ch1, 1tr in next tr, *(ch1, 1tr in next ch-3 sp) twice, ch1, 1tr in next tr; rep from * to last ch-1 sp, ch1, 1tr in top of beg 3-ch, turn. [33 (45) tr, 32 (44) ch-1 sps, 1 ch-3 sp]

Row 59 Ch4, skip ch-1 sp, 1tr in next tr, *ch3, skip next ch-1 sp and tr, 1dc in next ch-1 sp, ch3, skip next tr and ch-1 sp, 1tr in next tr; rep from * to last ch-1 sp, ch3, skip ch-1 sp, ss in next tr, turn, ch3, skip ch-3 sp just made, ss to last tr of current row. [12 (16) tr, 10 (14) dc, 21 (29) ch-3 sps, 1 ch-1 sp]

Row 60 Ch3, skip next ch-3 sp and dc, 1tr in next ch-3 sp, ch1, 1tr in next tr, *(ch1, 1tr in next ch-3 sp) twice, ch1, 1tr in next tr, (ch1, tr in next ch-3 sp) twice, ch1, pc in next tr; rep from * to last 2 ch-3 sps, (ch1, 1tr in next ch-3 sp) twice, ch1, 1tr in next tr, ch1, 1tr in top of beg

3-ch, turn. [26 (36) tr, 4 (6) pc, 29 (41) ch-1 sps, 1 ch-3 sp]

Row 61 Rep Row 59. [11 (15) tr, 9 (13) dc, 19 (27) ch-3 sps, 1 ch-1 sp]

Row 62 Ch3, skip next ch-3 sp and dc, 1tr in next ch-3 sp, ch1, 1tr in next tr, *(ch1, 1tr in next ch-3 sp) twice, ch1, 1tr in next tr; rep from * to last ch-1 sp, ch1, 1tr in top of beg 3-ch, turn. [27 (39) tr, 26 (38) ch-1 sps, 1 ch-3 sp]

Row 63 Rep Row 59. [10 (14) tr, 8 (12) dc, 17 (25) ch-3 sps, 1 ch-1 sp]

Row 64 Ch3, skip ch-3 sp and dc, 1tr in next ch-3 sp, ch1, 1tr in next tr, (ch1, 1tr in next ch-3 sp) twice, ch1, pc in next tr, *(ch1, 1tr in next ch-3 sp) twice, ch1, 1tr in next tr, (ch1, 1tr in next ch-3 sp) twice, ch1, pc in next tr; rep from * to last sp, replacing last pc with 1tr, ch1, 1tr in top of beg 3-ch, turn. [21 (31) tr, 3 (5) pc, 23 (35) ch-1 sps, 1 ch-3 sp]

Row 65 Rep Row 59. [9 (13) tr, 7 (11) dc, 15 (23) ch-3 sps, 1 ch-1 sp]

STITCH CHART 2: SHAPING SHOULDERS ON FRONT RIGHT PANEL
Chart shows Size XS-M

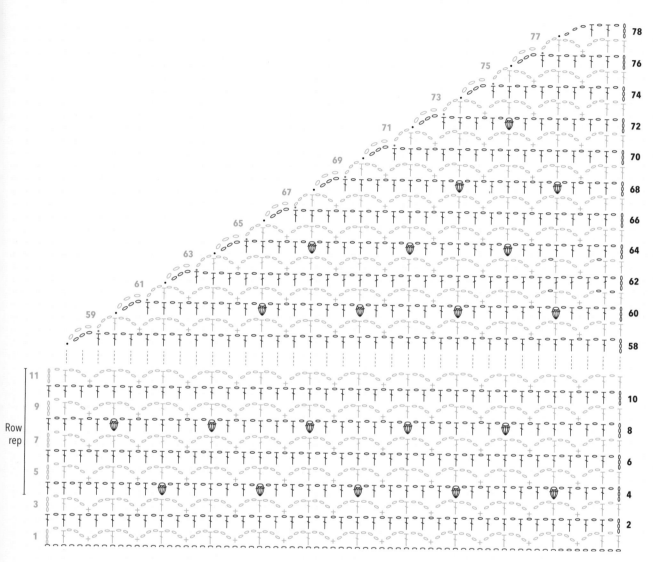

Row 66 Rep Row 62. [21 (33) tr, 20 (32) ch-1 sps, 1 ch-3 sp]

Row 67 Rep Row 59. [8 (12) tr, 6 (10) dc, 13 (21) ch-3 sps, 1 ch-1 sp]

Row 68 Rep Row 60. [16 (26) tr, 2 (4) pc, 17 (29) ch-1 sps, 1 ch-3 sp]

Row 69 Rep Row 59. [7 (11) tr, 5 (9) dc, 11 (19) ch-3 sps, 1 ch-1 sp]

Row 70 Rep Row 62. [15 (27) tr, 14 (26) ch-1 sps, 1 ch-3 sp]

Row 71 Rep Row 59. [6 (10) tr, 4 (8) dc, 9 (17) ch-3 sps, 1 ch-1 sp]

Row 72 Rep Row 64. [11 (21) tr, 1 (3) pc, 11 (23) ch-1 sps, 1 ch-3 sp]

Row 73 Rep Row 59. [5 (9) tr, 3 (7) dc, 7 (15) ch-3 sps, 1 ch-1 sp]

Row 74 Rep Row 62. [9 (21) tr, 8 (20) ch-1 sps, 1 ch-3 sp]

Row 75 Rep Row 59. [4 (8) tr, 2 (6) dc, 5 (13) ch-3 sps, 1 ch-1 sp]

Row 76 Rep Row 62. [6 (18) tr, 5 (17) ch-1 sps, 1 ch-3 sp]

Row 77 (Size XS-M) Ch4, skip ch-1 sp, 1tr in next tr, ch3, skip next ch-1 sp and tr, 1dc in next ch-1 sp, ch3, skip next tr and ch-1 sp, 1tr in next tr, ch3, skip ch-1 sp, ss in next tr, turn, ch3, skip ch-3 sp just made, ss to last tr of current row. [3 tr, 1 dc, 3 ch-3 sps, 1 ch-1 sp]

Row 77 (Size L-XXL) Rep Row 59. [7 tr, 5 dc, 11 ch-3 sps, 1 ch-1 sp]

Row 78 (Size XS-M) Ch3, skip next ch-3 sp and dc, 1tr in next ch-3 sp, ch1, 1tr in next tr, ch1, 1tr in top of beg 3-ch. Fasten off leaving 1m tail. [3 tr, 1 ch-3 sp, 2 ch-1 sps]

Row 78 (Size L-XXL) Rep Row 62. Fasten off leaving 1m tail. [15 tr, 14 ch-1 sps, 1 ch-3 sp]

FRONT RIGHT PANEL

With 5mm hook, ch74 (98), rep Rows 1-3 as for Front Left Panel. [14 (18) tr, 11 (15) dc, 22 (30) ch-3 sps, 2 ch-1 sps]

Row 4 Rep Row 8 of Front Left Panel.

Row 5 Rep Row 3 of Front Left Panel.

Row 6 Rep Row 2 of Front Left Panel.

Row 7 Rep Row 3 of Front Left Panel.

Row 8 Rep Row 4 of Front Left Panel.

Row 9 Rep Row 3 of Front Left Panel.

Row 10 Rep Row 2 of Front Left Panel.

Row 11 Rep Row 3 of Front Left Panel.

Rows 12-51 Rep Rows 4-11 five more times.

Rows 52-57 Rep Rows 4-9 once.

Shape Shoulder

Rows 58-78 Follow either written instructions below or Stitch Chart 2 for shaping shoulder. *Note: Chart shows Size XS-M. Size L-XXL will have more sts left after Row 78.*

Row 58 Ch4, skip ch-1 sp, 1tr in next tr, *(ch1, 1tr in next ch-3 sp) twice, ch1, 1tr in next tr; rep from * to last 2 ch-3 sps, ch1, 1tr in next ch-3 sp, ch3, skip next dc and ch-3 sp, ss in next tr, turn, ch3, skip ch-3 sp just made, ss to last tr of current row. [33 (45) tr, 32 (44) ch-1 sps, 1 ch-3 sp]

Row 59 Ch3, skip ch-1 sp, 1tr in next tr, *ch3, skip next ch-1 sp and tr, 1dc in next ch-1 sp, ch3, skip next tr and ch-1 sp, 1tr in next tr; rep from * to last ch-1 sp, ch1, 1tr in top of beg 3-ch, turn. [12 (16) tr, 10 (14) dc, 21 (29) ch-3 sps, 1 ch-1 sp]

Row 60 Ch4, skip ch-1 sp, 1tr in next tr, (ch1, 1tr in next ch-3 sp) twice, ch1, pc in next tr, *(ch1, 1tr in next ch-3 sp) twice, ch1, 1tr in next tr, (ch1, 1tr in next ch-3 sp) twice, ch1, pc in next tr; rep from * to last 2 ch-3 sps replacing last pc with 1tr, ch1, 1tr in next ch-3 sp, ch3, skip next dc and ch-3 sp, ss to last tr of prev row, turn, ch3, skip ch-3 sp just made, ss to last tr of current row. [26 (36) tr, 4 (6) pc, 29 (41) ch-1 sps, 1 ch-3 sp]

Row 61 Rep Row 59. [11 (15) tr, 9 (13) dc, 19 (27) ch-3 sps, 1 ch-1 sp]

Row 62 Rep Row 58. [27 (39) tr, 26 (38) ch-1 sps, 1 ch-3 sp]

Row 63 Rep Row 59. [10 (14) tr, 8 (12) dc, 17 (25) ch-3 sps, 1 ch-1 sp]

Row 64 Ch4, skip ch-1 sp, 1tr in next tr, (ch1, 1tr in next ch-3 sp) twice, ch1, 1tr in next tr, *(ch1, 1tr in next ch-3 sp) twice, ch1, pc in next tr, (ch1, 1tr in next ch-3 sp) twice, ch1, 1tr in next tr; rep from * to last 2 ch-3 sps, ch1, 1tr in next ch-3 sp, ch3, skip next dc and ch-3 sp, ss to last tr of prev row, turn, ch3, skip ch-3 sp just made, ss to last tr of current row. [21 (31) tr, 3 (5) pc, 23 (35) ch-1 sps, 1 ch-3 sp]

Row 65 Rep Row 59. [9 (13) tr, 7 (11) dc, 15 (23) ch-3 sps, 1 ch-1 sp]

Row 66 Rep Row 58. [21 (33) tr, 20 (32) ch-1 sps, 1 ch-3 sp]

Row 67 Rep Row 59. [8 (12) tr, 6 (10) dc, 13 (21) ch-3 sps, 1 ch-1 sp]

Row 68 Rep Row 60. [16 (26) tr, 2 (4) pc, 17 (29) ch-1 sps, 1 ch-3 sp]

Row 69 Rep Row 59. [7 (11) tr, 5 (9) dc, 11 (19) ch-3 sps, 1 ch-1 sp]

Row 70 Rep Row 58. [15 (27) tr, 14 (26) ch-1 sps, 1 ch-3 sp]

Row 71 Rep Row 59. [6 (10) tr, 4 (8) dc, 9 (17) ch-3 sps, 1 ch-1 sp]

Row 72 Rep Row 64. [11 (21) tr, 1 (3) pc, 11 (23) ch-1 sps, 1 ch-3 sp]

Row 73 Rep Row 59. [5 (9) tr, 3 (7) dc, 7 (15) ch-3 sps, 1 ch-1 sp]

Row 74 Rep Row 58. [9 (21) tr, 8 (20) ch-1 sps, 1 ch-3 sp]

Row 75 Rep Row 59. [4 (8) tr, 2 (6) dc, 5 (13) ch-3 sps, 1 ch-1 sp]

Row 76 Rep Row 58. [6 (18) tr, 5 (17) ch-1 sps, 1 ch-3 sp]

Row 77 (Size XS-M) Ch3, skip ch-1 sp, 1tr in next tr, ch3, skip next ch-1 sp and tr, 1dc in next ch-1 sp, ch3, skip next tr and ch-1 sp, 1tr in next tr, ch1, 1tr in top of beg 3-ch, turn. [7 tr, 5 dc, 11 ch-3 sps, 1 ch-1 sp]

Row 77 (Size L-XXL) Rep Row 59. [7 tr, 5 dc, 11 ch-3 sps, 1 ch-1 sp]

Row 78 (Size XS-M) Ch4, skip ch-1 sp, 1tr in next tr, ch1, 1tr in next ch-3 sp, ch3, skip next dc and ch-3 sp, ss to next tr. Fasten off leaving 1m tail. [3 tr, 1 ch-3 sp, 2 ch-1 sps]

Row 78 (Size L-XXL) Rep Row 58. Fasten off leaving 1m tail. [15 tr, 14 ch-1 sps, 1 ch-3 sp]

Block both panels to 35 (47) cm wide x 78cm high at longest edge.

BACK

With 5mm hook, ch176 (224), rep Rows 1-3 as for Front Left Panel. [31 (39) tr, 28 (36) dc, 56 (72) ch-3 sps, 2 ch-1 sps]

Row 4 Ch4, skip ch-1 sp, 1tr in next tr, *(ch1, 1tr in next ch-3 sp) twice, ch1, 1tr in next tr, (ch1, 1tr in next ch-3 sp) twice, ch1, pc in next tr; rep from * to last ch-1 sp, replacing last pc with 1tr, ch1, 1tr in top of beg 3-ch, turn. [74 (94) tr, 13 (17) pc, 86 (110) ch-1 sps]

Row 5 Rep Row 3.

Row 6 Rep Row 2. [87 (111) tr, 86 (110) ch-1 sps]

Row 7 Rep Row 3.

Row 8 Ch4, skip ch-1 sp, 1tr in next tr, (ch1, 1tr in next ch-3 sp) twice, ch1, pc in next tr, *(ch1, 1tr in next ch-3 sp) twice, ch1, 1tr in next tr, (ch1, 1tr in next ch-3 sp) twice, ch1, pc in next tr; rep from * to last 2 ch-3 sps, (ch1, 1tr in next ch-3 sp) twice, ch1, 1tr in next tr, ch1, 1tr in top of beg 3-ch, turn. [73 (93) tr, 14 (18) pc, 86 (110) ch-1 sps]

Row 9 Rep Row 3.

Row 10 Rep Row 2. [87 (111) tr, 86 (110) ch-1 sps]

Row 11 Rep Row 3.

Rows 12-51 Rep Rows 4-11 five more times.

Rows 52-57 Rep Rows 4-9 once.

Shape Shoulders

Rows 58-78 Follow either written instructions below or both Stitch Charts 1 and 2. *Note: You should follow decs on each side, and middle of back should be made with same st patt as before. Chart shows Size XS-M. Size L-XXL will have more sts left after Row 78.*

Row 58 Ch3, skip ch-1 sp, ss in next tr, ch3, skip next ch-3 sp and dc, 1tr in next ch-3 sp, ch1, 1tr in next tr, *(ch1, 1tr in next ch-3 sp) twice, ch1, 1tr in next tr; rep from * to last 2 ch-3 sps, ch1, 1tr in next ch-3 sp, ch3, skip next dc and ch-3 sp, ss in next tr, turn, ch3, skip ch-3 sp just made, ss to last tr of current row. [81 (105) tr, 80 (104) ch-1 sps, 2 ch-3 sps]

Row 59 Ch3, skip ch-1 sp, 1tr in next tr, *ch3, skip next ch-1 sp and tr, 1dc in next ch-1 sp, ch3, skip next tr and ch-1 sp, 1tr in next tr; rep from * to last ch-1 sp, ch3, skip ch-1 sp, ss in next tr, turn, ch3, skip ch-3 sp just made, ss to last tr of current row. [27 (35) tr, 26 (34) dc, 54 (70) ch-3 sps]

Row 60 Ch3, skip next ch-3 sp and dc, 1tr in next ch-3 sp, ch1, 1tr in next tr, *(ch1, 1tr in next ch-3 sp) twice, ch1, 1tr in next tr, (ch1, 1tr in next ch-3 sp) twice, ch1, pc in next tr; rep from * to last two ch-3 sps, replacing last pc with 1tr, ch1, 1tr in next ch-3 sp, ch3, skip next dc and ch-3 sp, ss to last tr of prev row, turn, ch3, skip ch-3 sp just made, ss to last tr of current row. [64 (84) tr, 11 (15) pc, 74 (98) ch-1 sps, 2 ch-3 sps]

Row 61 Rep Row 59. [25 (33) tr, 24 (32) dc, 50 (66) ch-3 sps]

Row 62 Ch3, skip next ch-3 sp and dc, 1tr in next ch-3 sp, ch1, 1tr in next tr, *(ch1, 1tr in next ch-3 sp) twice, ch1, 1tr in next tr; rep from * to last two ch-3 sps, ch1, 1tr in next ch-3 sp, ch3, skip next dc and ch-3 sp, ss in next tr, turn, ch3, skip ch-3 sp just made, ss to last tr of current row. [69 (93) tr, 68 (92) ch-1 sps, 2 ch-3 sps]

Row 63 Rep Row 59. [23 (31) tr, 22 (30) dc, 46 (62) ch-3 sps]
Row 64 Ch3, skip ch-3 sp and dc, 1tr in next ch-3 sp, ch1, 1tr in next tr, *(ch1, 1tr in next ch-3 sp) twice, ch1, pc in next tr, (ch1, 1tr in next ch-3 sp) twice, ch1, 1tr in next tr; rep from * to last two ch-3 sps, ch1, 1tr in next ch-3 sp, ch3, skip next dc and ch-3 sp, ss to last tr of prev row, turn, ch3, skip ch-3 sp just made, ss to last tr of current row. [53 (73) tr, 10 (14) pc, 62 (86) ch-1 sps, 2 ch-3 sps]
Row 65 Rep Row 59. [21 (29) tr, 20 (28) dc, 42 (58) ch-3 sps]
Row 66 Rep Row 62. [57 (81) tr, 56 (80) ch-1 sps, 2 ch-3 sps]
Row 67 Rep Row 59. [19 (27) tr, 18 (26) dc, 38 (54) ch-3 sps]
Row 68 Rep Row 60. [44 (64) tr, 7 (11) pc, 50 (74) ch-1 sps, 2 ch-3 sps]
Row 69 Rep Row 59. [17 (25) tr, 16 (24) dc, 34 (50) ch-3 sps]
Row 70 Rep Row 62. [45 (69) tr, 54 (68) ch-1 sps, 2 ch-3 sps]
Row 71 Rep Row 59. [15 (23) tr, 14 (22) dc, 30 (46) ch-3 sps]
Row 72 Rep Row 64. [33 (53) tr, 6 (10) pc, 38 (62) ch-1 sps, 2 ch-3 sps]
Row 73 Rep Row 59. [13 (21) tr, 12 (20) dc, 26 (42) ch-3 sps]
Row 74 Rep Row 62. [33 (57) tr, 32 (56) ch-1 sps, 2 ch-3 sps]
Row 75 Rep Row 59. [11 (19) tr, 10 (18) dc, 22 (38) ch-3 sps]
Row 76 Rep Row 62. [27 (51) tr, 26 (50) ch-1 sps, 2 ch-3 sps]
Row 77 Rep Row 59. [9 (17) tr, 8 (16) dc, 18 (34) ch-3 sps]
Row 78 Ch3, skip next ch-3 sp and dc, 1tr in next ch-3 sp, ch1, 1tr in next tr, *(ch1, 1tr in next ch-3 sp) twice, ch1, 1tr in next tr; rep from * to last two ch-3 sps, ch1, 1tr in next ch-3 sp, ch3, skip next dc and ch-3 sp, ss to next tr. Fasten off.
Block Back to 86 (110)cm wide x 78cm high at centre.

HEM AND SIDE EDGE
Sew shoulder seams using yarn ends.
With Front Left Panel facing, attach yarn with ss in first foundation ch at bottom of panel in centre.
Row 1 (RS) With 5.5mm hook, ch1, 1dc in same ch, *2dc in next sp, 3dc in next sp; rep from * to cnr, (1dc, ch2, 1dc) in last foundation ch, rotate work 90 degrees and cont along side of Front Left Panel and side of Back as folls: **1dc in next sp, 2dc in next sp; rep from ** to next cnr, (1dc, ch2, dc1) in first foundation ch of Back, rotate work 90 degrees and cont along bottom of Back as folls: ***2dc in next sp, 3dc in next sp; rep from *** to next cnr, (1dc, ch2, 1dc) in last foundation ch of Back, rotate work 90 degrees and cont along other side of Back and Front Right Panel as folls: ****1dc in next sp, 2dc in next sp; rep from **** to next cnr, (1dc, ch2, 1dc) in first foundation ch of Front Right Panel, rotate work 90 degrees and cont along bottom of Front Right Panel as folls: *****2dc in next sp, 3dc in next sp; rep from ***** to last cnr, 1dc in last foundation ch, turn.
Row 2 (WS) Ch1 (does not count as st throughout), 1dc blo in same st, *1dc blo in each st to cnr ch-2 sp, (1dc, ch2, 1dc) in ch-2 sp; rep from * along all sides ending with 1dc in last st instead of increasing, turn.
Rows 3-4 Rep Row 2.
PMs on Row 4 in st in line with shoulders on both Left and Right Panel, then count 30 sts down from markers on both Front Panels, place another marker for buttonhole. Remove markers at shoulder seams.

Row 5 (buttonhole row) Ch1, 1dc blo in same st, 1dc blo in each st to cnr ch-2 sp, (1dc, ch2, 1dc) in ch-2 sp, 1dc blo in each st to 1 st before marked st, ch2, skip 2 sts, cont with 1dc blo in each st and (1dc, ch2, 1dc) in each ch-2 sp to next marked st, ch2, skip 2 sts, 1dc blo in each st to last cnr ch-2 sp, (1dc, ch2, 1dc) in ch-2 sp, 1dc blo in each st to end.
Row 6 Rep Row 2 but work 2dc in each buttonhole ch-2 sp.
Row 7 Rep Row 2, but work (1dc, 2ch, 1dc) in last st, rotate work 90 degrees to cont with collar.

COLLAR
Collar is worked along inside edges of both front panels and across neck opening on back.
Row 1 (RS) 5dc evenly along side of hem, *1dc in next sp, 2dc in next sp; rep from * up right panel edge, across back neck and down left panel edge to hem, 5dc evenly along side of hem, turn.
Row 2 (WS) Ch1, 1dc blo in same st, 1dc blo in each st to end, turn.
Rep Row 2 until collar measures approx. 15cm, fasten off.

TO FINISH
Weave in all ends. Block to measurements. Sew on buttons.

SAFFRON WRAP
By Maria McPherson
justahappyhooker.blogspot.com

MEASUREMENTS
55 x 170cm (21.5 x 67in)
after blocking

ABBREVIATIONS
See back cover flap

MATERIALS
Scheepjes Whirl Ombré (60% Cotton, 40% Acrylic; 215g/1000m)
564 Golden Glowworm x 1 yarn cake
3.5mm crochet hook
Toho Beads, no. TH8-0302 x 100g
Fine long eye needle for threading beads

GAUGE/TENSION
A single motif measures 9 x 9cm using a 3.5mm hook after blocking.

SPECIAL ABBREVIATIONS
2tr-cl 2 treble crochet cluster stitch: (yoh, insert hook in st/sp, yoh, pull up lp, yoh, draw through 2 lps) twice in same st/sp (3 lps on hook), yoh, draw through all lps
3tr-cl 3 treble crochet cluster stitch: (yoh, insert hook in st/sp, yoh, pull up lp, yoh, draw through 2 lps) 3 times in same st/sp (4 lps on hook), yoh, draw through all lps
beg-cl beginning cluster: 1tr (ch3) used at start of first cluster in round
pb place bead by sliding along yarn to hook, work over bead in next st

PATTERN NOTES
This is a Join As You Go (JAYG) construction. The first motif is worked in its entirety. Subsequent motifs are joined together on Round 3 as per Joining Instructions and Schematic. There are 6 motifs per row, and 19 rows. Make 114 motifs in total.
Colour changes within the yarn can be slightly bumpy. Carefully trim any excess fuzz without damaging the integrity of the yarn to enable beads to run smoothly.

INSTRUCTIONS

MOTIF
Thread 32 beads onto yarn.
Ch5, ss to first ch to join into a ring.
Round 1 (RS) Ch3 (counts as beg-cl throughout), work into ring:
1tr, pb, ch3, pb, (2tr-cl, pb, ch3, pb) 7 times, ss to top of beg-cl to join.
[16 beads, 8 2tr-cl, 8 ch-3 sps]
Round 2 Ss into next ch-sp, ch3, 2tr-cl in same ch-sp, pb, ch4, pb, (3tr-cl in next ch-sp, pb, ch4, pb) 7 times, ss to top of beg-cl.
[16 beads, 8 3tr-cl, 8 ch-4 sps]
Round 3 *Note: Work this round for first motif; for subsequent motifs this is the joining round and is worked according to Joining Instructions and Schematic.*

Ss into next ch-sp, ch4 (counts as 1 dtr), 4dtr in same ch-sp, ch7 (cnr), 5dtr in next ch-sp, ch3, (5dtr in next ch-sp, ch7 (cnr), 5dtr in next ch-sp, ch3) 3 times, ss to top of beg 4-ch. Fasten off and weave in ends.

JOINING INSTRUCTIONS
Follow Joining Schematic.
Motifs are joined tog in ch-sps, as shown by red arrows.
To join in a ch-3 sp, ch1, slip hook under ch-3 sp of adjoining motif, ch1 over join, ch1.
To join in a ch-7 sp, ch3, slip hook under ch-7 sp of adjoining motif, ch1 over join, ch3.
To achieve a neat join where 4 cnrs meet, join diagonal cnrs tog as per Schematic.

TO FINISH
Weave in all ends and wet block to measurements.

STITCH CHART 1: MOTIF

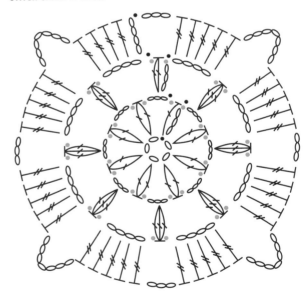

KEY

•	ss	✦	3tr-cl
•	pb		
⬭	ch	⊤	dtr
⬧	2tr-cl		

SCHEMATIC 1: JOINS AND JOINING SEQUENCE

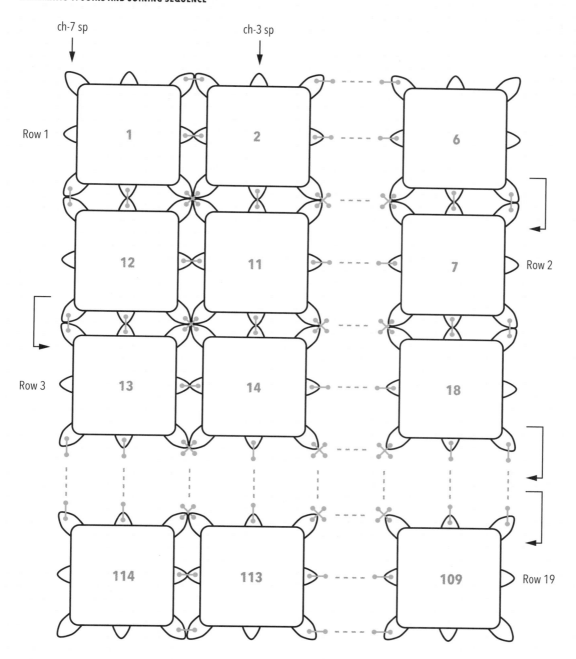

BLOOMING TEA COSY
By Christa Veenstra
thecuriocraftsroom.blogspot.com

MEASUREMENTS
Panel height 11cm (4.3in)
Bottom width 22cm (8.8in)
Top width 16cm (6.3in)

ABBREVIATIONS
See back cover flap

MATERIALS
Scheepjes Catona (100% Mercerised Cotton; 25g/62.5m)
Yarn A: 394 Shadow Purple x 3 balls
Yarn B: 240 Amethyst x 1 ball
Yarn C: 401 Dark Teal x 1 ball
Yarn D: 528 Silver Blue x 1 ball
2mm crochet hook
2.5mm crochet hook
3.5mm crochet hook
Sewing thread
Sewing needle
8mm press fastener
Teapot, circumference bottom 46cm (18in), circumference top 32cm (12.5in), height 11cm (4.3in)

GAUGE/TENSION
22 sts and 24 rows to measure 10 x 10cm over Panel patt using a 2.5mm hook.

MEASUREMENTS
Large Star Top from point to point without edging 14cm (5.5in)
Small Star Top from point to point without edging 11cm (4.3in)
Flower from point to point 6cm (2.3in)

SPECIAL ABBREVIATIONS
etr extended treble crochet: yoh, insert hook into st, pull up lp, yoh, draw through 1 lp on hook, (yoh, draw through 2 lps on hook) twice
picot ch2 ch2, ss in second ch from hook
picot ch3 ch3, ss in third ch from hook

PATTERN NOTES
This Tea Cosy consists of 2 panels that fit around the teapot, 2 stars that form the top, and 5 flowers. After finishing all sections, the Tea Cosy is sewn together.
Panels are worked back and forth in rows; turn at end of each row.
When working ttr on WS of panels, make sure the little bobbles lie on RS, not WS.

INSTRUCTIONS

PANEL AROUND TEAPOT (MAKE 2)
With 3.5mm hook and Yarn A, ch45.
Change to 2.5mm hook.
Row 1 (RS) Ch1 (does not count as st throughout), 1dc in second ch from hook and in each ch to end, turn. [45 dc]
Row 2 (WS) Ch1, 1dc in first dc, *1ttr, 1dc; rep from * to end, turn.

[23 dc, 22 ttr]
Row 3 Ch1, 1dc in each st to end. [45 dc]
Note: If you look at WS, you will see a neat row of horizontal 'V' lps; work 1dc in each of these lps.
Row 4 Ch1, 1ttr in first dc, 1dc, *1ttr, 1dc; rep from * to last dc, (1ttr, 1dc) in last dc. [23 dc, 23 ttr]
Row 5 Ch1, skip 1 dc, 1dc in next ttr and in each st to end. [45 dc]
Rows 6-12 Rep Rows 2-5 once then Rows 2-4 once.
Row 13 Ch1, skip 1 dc, dc2tog over ttr and dc, 1dc in next st and each st to last 2 sts, dc2tog over dc and ttr. [43 sts]
Row 14 Rep Row 4. [1 st inc]
Row 15 Rep Row 13. [3 sts dec]
Note: After each rep of Row 4 and Row 13, st count will decrease by a total of 2 sts.
Rows 16-25 Rep Rows 14 and 15 a total of 5 more times, do not fasten off. [31 sts]

PANEL EDGING ON LEFT-HAND SIDE
Rotate work 90 degrees.
Edge Row 1dc in side of dc2tog just made (do not start row with ch1), *1dc in side of next row end; rep from * to bottom of panel, fasten off leaving a long tail. [25 dc]
Note: The exact number of dc sts is not important, as long as there is a neat edge.

PANEL EDGING ON RIGHT-HAND SIDE
With RS facing, join Yarn A with 1dc in bottom row end of right-hand side of panel, *1dc in side of next row end; rep from * to top of panel, fasten off leaving a long tail. [25 dc]

LARGE STAR TOP
With 2mm hook and Yarn B, make a magic ring leaving a long tail.
Note: Leave large opening because a total of 30 tr are worked into ring and opening needs to fit over knob of lid. Only secure magic ring after making sure opening fits over knob.
Round 1 Ch2 (counts as first tr), 29tr in ring, ss to beg 2-ch to join. [30 tr]
Round 2 Ch3 (counts as first tr throughout), (2tr in next tr, 4tr) 5 times, 2tr in next tr, 3tr, ss to beg 3-ch. [36 tr]
Round 3 Ch3, (2tr in next tr, 2tr) 11 times, 2tr in next tr, 1tr, ss to beg 3-ch. [48 tr]
Round 4 Ch3, (2tr in next tr, 3tr) 11 times, 2tr in next tr, 2tr, ss to beg 3-ch. [60 tr]
Round 5 Ch3, (2tr in next tr, 4tr) 11 times, 2tr in next tr, 3tr, ss to beg 3-ch. [72 tr]
Round 6 Ch1 (does not count as st throughout), 1dc in same tr, 2ss,

82 | PATTERNS

*1dc, 1htr, 1tr, 1etr, 3dtr in next tr, ch1, 3dtr in next tr, 1etr, 1tr, 1htr**, 1dc, 2ss; rep from * 5 more times ending last rep at **, ss to first dc. [36 dtr, 12 etr, 12 tr, 12 htr, 12 dc, 12 ss, 6 ch-1 sps]

Round 7 Ch1, 1dc in same dc, *2ss, 4dc, 1htr, (2tr in next st) twice, (1etr, ch2, 1etr) in ch-1 sp, (2tr in next st) twice, 1htr, 4dc; rep from * 5 more times ending last rep with 3dc, close with invisible join, fasten off. [12 etr, 48 tr, 12 htr, 48 dc, 12 ss, 6 ch-2 sps]
Change to 2.5mm hook.

Round 8 With Yarn A, starting in any ch-2 sp, ((1dc, ch2, 1dc) in ch-2 sp, 22ss blo) 6 times, close with invisible join, fasten off. [12 dc, 6 ch-2 sps, 132 ss blo]

Round 9 With Yarn C, starting in any ch-2 sp, *(1ss, ch2, 1ss) in ch-2 sp, ch9, skip (1 dc, 10 ss blo), 2ss blo, ch9; rep from * 5 more times, ss to first ss, fasten off. [12 ss, 12 ss blo, 6 ch-2 sps, 12 ch-9 sps]

Round 10 With Yarn D, starting in any ch-2 sp, *(1ss, picot ch3, 1ss) in ch-2 sp, ch9, 1ss blo in each of the 2 ss blo, ch9; rep from * 5 more times, ss to first ss, fasten off. [12 ss, 12 ss blo, 6 picot ch3, 12 ch-9 sps]
Weave in all ends.

SMALL STAR TOP

With 2mm hook and Yarn A, make a magic ring leaving a long tail.
Note: As for Large Top, leave a large opening.
Round 1 Ch2 (counts as first tr), 29tr in ring, ss to beg 2-ch to join. [30 tr]
Round 2 Ch3 (counts as first tr throughout), (2tr in next tr, 4tr) 5 times, 2tr in next tr, 3tr, ss to beg 3-ch. [36 tr]
Round 3 Ch3, (2tr in next tr, 2tr) 11 times, 2tr in next tr, 1tr, ss to beg 3-ch. [48 tr]
Round 4 Ch1 (does not count as st throughout), 1dc in same tr, 2ss, *1dc, 1htr, 3tr in next tr, ch1, 3tr in next tr, 1htr**, 1dc, 2ss; rep from * 5 more times ending last rep at **, ss to first dc. [36 tr, 12 htr, 12 dc, 12 ss, 6 ch-1 sps]
Round 5 Ch1, 1dc in same dc, *2ss, 3dc, 2htr in next st, (1htr, 1tr) in next st, (1tr, ch2, 1tr) in ch-1 sp, (1tr, 1htr) in next st, 2htr in next st, 3dc; rep from * 5 more times ending last rep with 2dc, close with invisible join, fasten off. [24 tr, 36 htr, 36 dc, 12 ss, 6 ch-2 sps]
Change to 2.5mm hook.
Round 6 With Yarn C, starting in any ch-2 sp, ((1dc, ch2, 1dc) in ch-2 sp, 18ss blo) 6 times, close with invisible join, fasten off. [12 dc, 6 ch-2 sps, 108 ss blo]
Round 7 With Yarn D, starting in any ch-2 sp, *(1ss, picot ch3, 1ss) in ch-2 sp, ch7, skip (1 dc, 8 ss blo), 2ss blo, ch7; rep from * 5 more times, ss to first ss, fasten off. [12 ss, 12 ss blo, 6 picot ch3, 12 ch-7 sps]
Weave in all ends.

FLOWER (MAKE 5)

With 2.5mm hook and Yarn B, make a magic ring.
Round 1 (1dc, ch2) 6 times into ring, ss to first dc to join, fasten off. [6 dc, 6 ch-2 sps]
Round 2 With Yarn D, 1ss in any dc, *ch2, (1tr, ch2, 1tr) in ch-2 sp, ch2, 1ss in dc; rep from * 5 more times omitting final ss on last rep, ss to first ss, fasten off. [6 ss, 12 tr, 18 ch-2 sps]
Round 3 With Yarn C, 1dc in any ss, *ch2, (1dc, picot ch2, 1dc) in ch-2

sp, ch2, 1dc in ss; rep from * 5 more times omitting final ss on last rep, ss to first dc, fasten off. [18 dc, 12 ch-2 sps, 6 picot ch2]
Weave in all ends and block to measurements.

TO FINISH

Place panels with WS tog and RS facing out. With tail end at top of panels on one side, whip stitch through a few edging sts up to spout. Rep for bottom of panels. With tail end at top of other side, whip stitch through a few edging sts up to handle. Try panels around teapot to make sure they fit snuggly, adjust if necessary. Sew press fastener onto bottom cnrs below handle.

Place small top over large top and pin into place. With Yarn A, top stitch small top onto large top around middle opening, then sew each of 6 points of small top into place and sew 3 flowers around middle opening, using photos as a guide.

Fit panels around teapot and place top section on top of teapot and pin into place. Remove cosy from teapot and with Yarn A, sew each point of top to panels.

With Yarn C, join rem 2 flowers to large top points at side of cosy by sewing them to picot ch3 of edging. Weave in all ends.

PETALS & LEAVES SHAWL
By Johanna Lindahl
mijocrochet.se

MEASUREMENTS
200 x 145 x 145cm
(79 x 57 x 57in)
after blocking

ABBREVIATIONS
See back cover flap

MATERIALS
Scheepjes Whirligig (20% Alpaca, 80% Virgin Wool; 450g/1000m)
201 Grey to Lavender x 1 yarn cake
5mm crochet hook

GAUGE/TENSION
15 sts and 7 rows to measure 10 x 10cm over tr using a 5mm hook.

SPECIAL ABBREVIATIONS
puff (yoh, insert hook in st, yoh, pull up lp) 3 times, yoh, draw through all lps, close puff with ch1

PATTERN NOTES
This pattern is worked in rows from top down.
Turn work at end of each row.

INSTRUCTIONS

Row 1 (WS) Ch5, (1tr, ch2, 1tr, ch1, 1tr) in fifth ch from hook (skipped 4 ch count as 1 tr and 1 ch). [4 tr, 2 ch-1 sps, 1 ch-2 sp]
Row 2 (RS) Ch3 (counts as 1 tr throughout), 1tr in st at base of ch, 3tr in next ch-1 sp, 1tr in next tr, (1tr, ch2, 1tr) in next ch-2 sp, 1tr in next tr, 3tr in next ch-1 sp, 2tr in last tr. [14 tr, 1 ch-2 sp]
Row 3 Ch4 (counts as 1 tr and 1 ch throughout), 1tr in next tr, ch1, skip 1 tr, (1tr, ch1, 1tr) in next tr, ch1, skip 1 tr, 1tr in next tr, ch1, skip 1 tr, (1tr, ch2, 1tr) in next ch-2 sp, ch1, skip 1 tr, 1tr in next tr, ch1, skip 1 tr, (1tr, ch1, 1tr) in next tr, ch1, skip 1 tr, 1tr in next tr, ch1, 1tr in last tr. [12 tr, 10 ch-1 sps, 1 ch-2 sp]
Row 4 Ch3, 1tr in st at base of ch, 3tr in next ch-1 sp, 1tr in next tr, ch1, skip (ch-1 sp, 1 tr), 1dc in next ch-1 sp, ch1, skip (1 tr, ch-1 sp), 1tr in next tr, 3tr in next ch-1 sp, 1tr in next tr, (1tr, ch2, 1tr) in next ch-2 sp, 1tr in next tr, 3tr in next ch-1 sp, 1tr in next tr, ch1, skip (ch-1 sp, 1 tr), 1dc in next ch-1 sp, ch1, skip (1 tr, ch-1 sp), 1tr in next tr, 3tr in next ch-1 sp, 2tr in last tr. [24 tr, 2 dc, 4 ch-1 sps, 1 ch-2 sp]
Row 5 Ch4, 1tr in next tr, ch1, skip 1 tr, (1tr, ch1, 1tr) in next tr, ch1, skip 1 tr, 1tr in next tr, ch1, skip (ch-1 sp, 1 dc, ch-1 sp), 1tr in next tr, ch1, skip 1 tr, (1tr, ch1, 1tr) in next tr, ch1, skip 1 tr, 1tr in next tr, ch1, skip 1 tr, (1tr, ch2, 1tr) in next ch-2 sp, ch1, skip 1 tr, 1tr in next tr, ch1, skip 1 tr, (1tr, ch1, 1tr) in next tr, ch1, skip 1 tr, 1tr in next tr, ch1, skip (ch-1 sp, 1 dc, ch-1 sp), 1tr in next tr, ch1, skip 1 tr, (1tr, ch1, 1tr) in next tr, ch1, skip 1 tr, 1tr in next tr, ch1, 1tr in last tr. [20 tr, 18 ch-1 sps, 1 ch-2 sp]
Row 6 Ch3, 1tr in st at base of ch, 3tr in next ch-1 sp, 1tr in next tr, *ch1, skip (ch-1 sp, 1 tr), 1dc in next ch-1 sp, ch1, skip (1 tr, ch-1 sp), 1tr in next tr, 3tr in next ch-1 sp, 1tr in next tr; rep from * to ch-2 sp, (1tr, ch2, 1tr) in ch-2 sp, 1tr in next tr, 3tr in next ch-1 sp, **1tr in next tr, ch1, skip (ch-1 sp, 1 tr), 1dc in next ch-1 sp, ch1, skip (1 tr, ch-1 sp), 1tr in next tr, 3tr in next ch-1 sp; rep from ** to last tr, 2tr in last tr. [34 tr, 4 dc, 8 ch-1 sps, 1 ch-2 sp]
Row 7 Ch4, 1tr in next tr, ch1, skip 1 tr, (1tr, ch1, 1tr) in next tr, ch1, skip 1 tr, 1tr in next tr, *ch1, skip (ch-1 sp, 1 dc, ch-1 sp), 1tr in next tr, ch1, skip 1 tr, (1tr, ch1, 1tr) in next tr, ch1, skip 1 tr, 1tr in next tr; rep from * to last tr before ch-2 sp, ch1, skip 1 tr, (1tr, ch2, 1tr) in ch-2 sp, ch1, skip 1 tr, 1tr in next tr, ch1, skip 1 tr, (1tr, ch1, 1tr) in next tr, ch1, skip 1 tr, 1tr in next tr, **ch1, skip (ch-1 sp, 1 dc, ch-1 sp), 1tr in next tr, ch1, skip 1 tr, (1tr, ch1, 1tr) in next tr, ch1, skip 1 tr, 1tr in next tr; rep from ** to last tr, ch1, 1tr in last tr. [28 tr, 26 ch-1 sps, 1 ch-2 sp]
Row 8 Rep Row 6. [44 tr, 6 dc, 12 ch-1 sps, 1 ch-2 sp]
Row 9 Ch4, (1FPtr in next tr, ch1) twice, skip 1 tr, 1FPtr in next tr, ch1, 1FPtr in next tr, *ch1, skip (ch-1 sp, 1 dc, ch-1 sp), (1FPtr in next tr, ch1) twice, skip 1 tr, 1FPtr in next tr, ch1, 1FPtr in next tr; rep from * to last tr before ch-2 sp, ch1, (1tr, ch2, 1tr) in ch-2 sp, (ch1, skip 1 tr, 1FPtr in next tr, ch1, 1FPtr in next tr) twice, **ch1, skip (ch-1 sp, 1 dc, ch-1 sp), (1FPtr in next tr, ch1) twice, skip 1 tr, 1FPtr in next tr, ch1, 1FPtr in next tr; rep from ** to last tr, ch1, 1tr in last tr. [4 tr, 32 FPtr, 34 ch-1 sps, 1 ch-2 sp]
Row 10 Rep Row 6. [54 tr, 8 dc, 16 ch-1 sps, 1 ch-2 sp]
Row 11 Rep Row 7. [44 tr, 42 ch-1 sps, 1 ch-2 sp]
Row 12 Rep Row 6. [64 tr, 10 dc, 20 ch-1 sps, 1 ch-2 sp]
Row 13 Rep Row 7. [52 tr, 50 ch-1 sps, 1 ch-2 sp]
Row 14 Rep Row 6. [74 tr, 12 dc, 24 ch-1 sps, 1 ch-2 sp]
Row 15 Rep Row 7. [60 tr, 58 ch-1 sps, 1 ch-2 sp]
Row 16 Rep Row 6. [84 tr, 14 dc, 28 ch-1 sps, 1 ch-2 sp]
Row 17 Rep Row 9. [4 tr, 64 FPtr, 66 ch-1 sps, 1 ch-2 sp]
Row 18 Rep Row 6. [94 tr, 16 dc, 32 ch-1 sps, 1 ch-2 sp]
Row 19 Rep Row 7. [76 tr, 74 ch-1 sps, 1 ch-2 sp]
Row 20 Rep Row 6. [104 tr, 18 dc, 36 ch-1 sps, 1 ch-2 sp]
Row 21 Rep Row 7. [84 tr, 82 ch-1 sps, 1 ch-2 sp]
Row 22 Rep Row 6. [114 tr, 20 dc, 40 ch-1 sps, 1 ch-2 sp]
Row 23 Rep Row 7. [92 tr, 90 ch-1 sps, 1 ch-2 sp]
Row 24 Rep Row 6. [124 tr, 22 dc, 44 ch-1 sps, 1 ch-2 sp]
Row 25 Rep Row 9. [4 tr, 96 FPtr, 98 ch-1 sps, 1 ch-2 sp]
Row 26 Rep Row 6. [134 tr, 24 dc, 48 ch-1 sps, 1 ch-2 sp]
Row 27 Rep Row 7. [108 tr, 106 ch-1 sps, 1 ch-2 sp]
Row 28 Rep Row 6. [144 tr, 26 dc, 52 ch-1 sps, 1 ch-2 sp]
Row 29 Rep Row 7. [116 tr, 114 ch-1 sps, 1 ch-2 sp]
Row 30 Rep Row 6. [154 tr, 28 dc, 56 ch-1 sps, 1 ch-2 sp]
Row 31 Rep Row 7. [124 tr, 122 ch-1 sps, 1 ch-2 sp]
Row 32 Rep Row 6. [164 tr, 30 dc, 60 ch-1 sps, 1 ch-2 sp]
Row 33 Rep Row 9. [4 tr, 128 FPtr, 130 ch-1 sps, 1 ch-2 sp]
Row 34 Rep Row 6. [174 tr, 32 dc, 64 ch-1 sps, 1 ch-2 sp]
Row 35 Rep Row 7. [140 tr, 138 ch-1 sps, 1 ch-2 sp]

Row 36 Rep Row 6. [184 tr, 34 dc, 68 ch-1 sps, 1 ch-2 sp]

Row 37 Rep Row 7. [148 tr, 146 ch-1 sps, 1 ch-2 sp]

Row 38 Rep Row 6. [194 tr, 36 dc, 72 ch-1 sps, 1 ch-2 sp]

Row 39 Rep Row 7. [156 tr, 154 ch-1 sps, 1 ch-2 sp]

Row 40 Rep Row 6. [204 tr, 38 dc, 76 ch-1 sps, 1 ch-2 sp]

Row 41 Rep Row 9. [4 tr, 160 FPtr, 162 ch-1 sps, 1 ch-2 sp]

Row 42 Rep Row 6. [214 tr, 40 dc, 80 ch-1 sps, 1 ch-2 sp]

Row 43 Rep Row 7. [172 tr, 170 ch-1 sps, 1 ch-2 sp]

Row 44 Rep Row 6. [224 tr, 42 dc, 84 ch-1 sps, 1 ch-2 sp]

Row 45 Rep Row 7. [180 tr, 178 ch-1 sps, 1 ch-2 sp]

Row 46 Rep Row 6. [234 tr, 44 dc, 88 ch-1 sps, 1 ch-2 sp]

Row 47 Rep Row 7. [188 tr, 186 ch-1 sps, 1 ch-2 sp]

Row 48 Rep Row 6. [244 tr, 46 dc, 92 ch-1 sps, 1 ch-2 sp]

Row 49 Ch3, 1FPtr in next 5 tr, *ch2, skip ch-1 sp, 1ss in next dc, ch2, skip ch-1 sp, 1FPtr in next 5 tr; rep from * to last tr before ch-2 sp, 1FPtr in next tr, (1tr, ch2, 1tr) in ch-2 sp, 1FPtr in next 6 tr, **ch2, skip ch-1 sp, 1ss in next dc, ch2, skip ch-1 sp, 1FPtr in next 5 tr; rep from ** to last tr, 1tr in last tr. [4 tr, 242 FPtr, 46 ss, 93 ch-2 sps]

Row 50 Ch1 (does not count as st), 1dc in st at base of ch, 1dc in next tr, 1puff in next tr, (1tr, ch2, 1tr) in next tr, 1puff in next tr, 1dc in next tr, *ch1, skip (ch-2 sp, 1 ss, ch-2 sp), 1dc in next tr, 1puff in next tr, (1tr, ch2, 1tr) in next tr, 1puff in next tr, 1dc in next tr; rep from * to last 2 tr before ch-2 sp at tip of shawl, ch1, skip 2 tr, (2tr, ch2, 2tr) in ch-2 sp, ch1, skip 2 tr, 1dc in next tr, 1puff in next tr, (1tr, ch2, 1tr) in next tr, 1puff in next tr, 1dc in next tr, **ch1, skip (ch-2 sp, 1 ss, ch-2 sp), 1dc in next tr, 1puff in next tr, (1tr, ch2, 1tr) in next tr, 1puff in next tr, 1dc in next tr; rep from ** to last tr, 1dc in last tr. [100 tr, 98 dc, 96 puffs, 48 ch-1 sps, 49 ch-2 sps]

Row 51 Ch3, 2tr in st at base of ch, skip 1 dc, 1tr in next puff, 1tr in next tr, (2tr, ch1, 2tr) in next ch-2 sp, 1tr in next tr, 1tr in next puff, *skip (1 dc, ch-1 sp, 1 dc), 1tr in next puff, 1tr in next tr, (2tr, ch1, 2tr) in next ch-2 sp, 1tr in next tr, 1tr in next puff; rep from * to last dc before ch-2 sp at tip of shawl, skip (1 dc, ch-1 sp), 1tr in next 2 tr, (2tr, ch2, 2tr) in ch-2 sp, 1tr in next 2 tr, skip (ch-1 sp, 1 dc), 1tr in next puff, 1tr in next tr, (2tr, ch1, 2tr) in next ch-2 sp, 1tr in next tr, 1tr in next puff, **skip (1 dc, ch-1 sp, 1 dc), 1tr in next puff, 1tr in next tr, (2tr, ch1, 2tr) in next ch-2 sp, 1tr in next tr, 1tr in next puff; rep from ** to last 2 dc, skip 1 dc, 3tr in last dc. [398 tr, 48 ch-1 sps, 1 ch-2 sp]

Row 52 Ch2, 1puff in st at base of ch, skip 1 tr, 1dc between next 2 tr, skip 1 tr, 1puff in next 2 tr, *2tr in next ch-1 sp, 1puff in next 2 tr, skip 1 tr, 1dc between next 2 tr, skip 1 tr, 1puff in next 2 tr; rep from * to ch-2 sp, 3tr in ch-2 sp, 1puff in next 2 tr, skip 1 tr, 1dc between next 2 tr, **skip 1 tr, 1puff in next 2 tr, 2tr in next ch-1 sp, 1puff in next 2 tr, skip 1 tr, 1dc between next 2 tr; rep from ** to last 2 tr, skip 1 tr, (1puff, ch2, 1ss) in last tr, fasten off. [99 tr, 50 dc, 198 puffs, 2 ch-2 sps, 1 ss]

TO FINISH

Weave in all ends, block to measurements.

EARL GREY SOCKS

By Carmen Jorissen
newleafdesigns.nl

MEASUREMENTS

See Measurements Table
and Pattern Notes

ABBREVIATIONS

See back cover flap

MATERIALS

Scheepjes Metropolis (75% Merino Extra Fine, 25% Nylon; 50g/200m)

Yarn A: 078 Lyon x 1 ball

Yarn B: 053 Santiago x 1 ball

Yarn C: 056 Almaty x 1 ball

Yarn D: 011 Boston x 1 ball

2.25mm circular needle, 80cm long, for toes, heels and cuffs

2.5mm circular needle, 80cm long, for colourwork section

Stitch marker

GAUGE/TENSION

34 sts and 36 rows to measure 10 x 10cm over Chart 1 using 2.5mm needles, unblocked.

PATTERN NOTES

These colourwork socks are knit from toe-up, using four colours. You can also knit them in just two colours. There are two colourwork charts: first sock uses Chart 1 for foot and Chart 2 for leg, second sock uses Chart 2 for foot and Chart 1 for leg. The magic loop method of working in the round will be used throughout.

Colourwork socks tend to have less stretch than regular socks, so make sure sock is wide enough for heel to pass through. If sock fits foot but is too snug for leg, use larger needle size for leg.

Make a swatch to check that your gauge matches gauge given. If you have more sts per 10cm, go up a needle size OR use more sts in sock circumference. If you have less sts per 10cm, go down a needle size OR use less sts in sock circumference. Colourwork chart works to rep of 10 sts, so only use a multiple of 10 sts. Refer to Measurements Table for number of recommended circumference sts for each size.

To ensure correct size for foot length, use Measurements Table to determine placement of heel. This measurement can be calculated as foot length minus 5cm (2in).

Sizing Instructions are given as 35-36 (37-38: 39-41: 42-43: 44-45: 46-47).

CHART 1

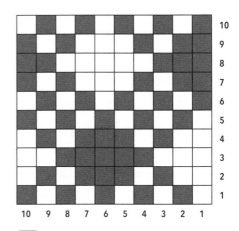

10 9 8 7 6 5 4 3 2 1

☐ Yarn A 078 Lyon

■ Yarn B 053 Santiago

CHART 2

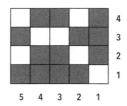

5 4 3 2 1

☐ Yarn C 056 Almaty

■ Yarn D 011 Boston

Measurements Table

Fits shoe size	Number of sts circumference	Knit until Toe + Foot together measure
EU 35-36	70	18cm (7in)
EU 37-38	70	19cm (7.5in)
EU 39-41	70	20cm (7.8in)
EU 42-43	80	21cm (8.3in)
EU 44-45	80	22cm (8.8in)
EU 46-47	80	23cm (9in)

INSTRUCTIONS

FIRST SOCK
TOE
With Yarn B and 2.25mm circular needle, cast on 12 sts on each needle using 'Judy's Magic Cast On'.
Round 1 K to end. [24 sts]
Round 2 (inc) (Kfb, k to last 2 sts on one needle, kfb, k1) twice. [4 sts inc]
Rep Round 2 a further 3 times. [40 sts]
Rep Rounds 1-2 until there are 68 (68: 68: 80: 80: 80) sts.
For first 3 sizes only:
Next round K to end.
Next round (inc) Kfb, k to last 2 sts on one needle, kfb, k1, k all sts on second needle. [70 sts]
Note: You will have 36 sts for front of foot, and 34 sts for sole. Mark side with 36 sts with stitch marker or scrap yarn.
All sizes:
Change to 2.5mm circular needle.
Using Yarns A and B, begin working from Chart 1 as folls:
Round 1 Work row 1 of Chart 1 a total of 7 (7: 7: 8: 8: 8) times around. Round 1 sets patt. Cont as set, working through rem rows in Chart 1, then rep Chart 1 until foot reaches desired length (see Measurements table), ending with either a row 4 or row 9.
Next round Work next 36 (36: 36: 40: 40: 40) instep sts from next row of Chart 1 (either row 5 or 10), change to 2.25mm circular needle and work rem 34 (34: 34: 40: 40: 40) heel sts in Yarn A, turn to work in rows. Fasten off Yarn B.

HEEL
Row 1 (WS) Wyif, sl1p and lift yarn from front upwards over right-hand needle all the way to back of work, tugging firmly (forms a 'double st'), p all heel sts, turn.
Row 2 (RS) Wyif, sl1p and lift yarn to back as before, k all sts up to next double st, turn.
Row 3 Wyif, sl1p and lift yarn to back as before, p all sts up to next double st, turn.
Rep Rows 2-3 until you have 16 sts (all sizes) left in between double sts, ending with a RS row, but DO NOT turn at end of last RS row, instead k following double st as if it were 1 st, turn.
Row 1 (WS) Sl1p, p to next double st, p as if it were 1 st, turn.
Row 2 (RS) Sl1p, k to next double st, k as if it were 1 st, turn.
Rep Rows 1-2 until all double sts have been worked and you have 34 (34: 34: 40: 40: 40) heel sts again, fasten off Yarn A.

LEG
Change to 2.5mm circular needle.
Using Yarns C and D, begin working from Chart 2 as folls:
Round 1 Work row 1 of Chart 2 a total of 7 (7: 7: 8: 8: 8) times around.
Note: If necessary to avoid gaps, pick up 1 st bet instep and sole and knit this st tog with next st. If needed, use a larger needle size for leg to create more room for ankle and instep.
Round 1 sets patt. Cont as set working through rem rows in Chart 2, then rep Chart 2 until leg measures approx. 13cm (5in) in length (you can knit longer legs but make sure socks fit around calves), ending with row 1 of Chart 2, fasten off Yarn C.

CUFF
Cont in Yarn D only.
Round 1 *K1, p1; rep from * to end.
Rep Round 1 a further 14 rounds.
Cast off loosely in rib.
Note: This cast off method is usually stretchy enough for colourwork socks. However, if cast off is too tight, try 'Jeny's Surprisingly Stretchy Bind-off'.

SECOND SOCK
Knit toe using Yarn D, then begin Chart 2 using Yarns C and D for foot. End last full round of Chart 2 with row 4, then knit across front in row 1 just before starting heel using Yarn D. After heel, begin Chart 1 using Yarns A and B, ending with a row 5 or 10. Work cuff using Yarn B.

TO FINISH
Wash and block to measurements, weave in all ends AFTER blocking.

LADY MABEL SWEATER

By Susan Walsh
peppergoose.design

MATERIALS

Scheepjes Our Tribe (70% Merino Superwash, 30% Polyamide; 100g/420m)
983 Motivate x 5 (5: 6: 7: 8) balls, plus 1 ball for swatching (see Pattern Notes)
3mm crochet hook
3.25mm crochet hook
3.5mm crochet hook
Stitch markers

GAUGE/TENSION

Main fabric: 29 sts and 22 rows to measure 10 x 10cm over alternating (1dc flo, ch1) using a 3.5mm hook, after blocking.

SPECIAL ABBREVIATIONS

Refer to Stitch Chart 1: Feature Panel.

cable ch3, skip 2 sts, 1dc in next st, turn, 1dc in each of 3 ch, 1ss in next dc, turn, 1dc in each of 2 skipped sts. *Note: Firm tension for '1dc in each of 3 ch' is required for a well-structured cable*

crossed-tr crossed treble crochet: 2tr in second next ch-sp, 2tr in skipped ch-sp, crossing over the 2 tr just made *Note: the 4 strands of yarn should line up at the back of crossed-tr*

ext ch extension chain: ch(s) worked at end of a row to form a base for next row

flat ss seam flat slip stitch seam: with RS tog, 1ss in outer lps of each aligned st to end

main fabric patt ch2 (counts as 1 dc and 1 ch), (1dc flo, ch1) in fifth st from hook and in each dc to last dc, 1dc flo in last dc

main fabric patt into 2 rows below ch2 (counts as 1 dc and 1 ch), working into the unworked lp of 2 rows below and starting in third st of row, (1dc flo, ch1) in every alt st to last st, 1dc flo in last st. *Note: This pushes prev ss row to form a ridge on RS of work (See Stitch Chart 1: Feature Panel).*

post tr a FPtr or BPtr (*See Standard Abbreviations and post ribbing join*)

post tr ribbing:

Round 1 (RS) Ch2 (counts as 1 tr), 1tr in each dc around, ss to first tr to join, turn

Round 2 (WS) Ch1 (does not count as st), (FPtr around next st, BPtr around next st) around to last st, post ribbing join, turn

Round 3 (RS) Ch1 (does not count as st), (BPtr around next st, FPtr around next st) around to last st, post ribbing join, turn
Last two rounds set patt. Cont in patt as set to complete specified total number of post ribbing rounds

post ribbing join work last post tr in ribbing patt of round to last 2 lps on hook, insert hook in beg tr of round, yoh, pull through tr and all lps on hook. *This ridge produces a ribbed look to both sides of work so parts can be joined invisibly*

secret sew finish cut yarn leaving a 20cm tail. Gently pull yarn through top of last st made at end of round/row. Thread yarn into tapestry needle, sew front to back under top 2 lps of second next st and sew back into top of last st made at end of round/row. Sew in loose end securely

ss row ch1 (counts as ss), 1ss flo in third st from hook and in each st to end

PATTERN NOTES

Back and Front pieces are made separately with rows oriented vertically, working from cuff to cuff. Crochet edging and flat ss seams are used to join Shoulder-Sleeve seams, then underarm/side seams to assemble bodice. Openings are edged in dc rounds with decreases, then post tr ribbing finishes the garment.

Before starting garment, work 2 swatches to check gauge and understanding of textured sts: 1 swatch in Main Fabric Pattern 30 rows x 41 sts wide, and 1 swatch in Initial Feature Panel Rows (as shown in Stitch Chart 1) x 41 sts wide.

MEASUREMENTS
See Measurements Table

ABBREVIATIONS
See back cover flap

Measurements Table

Size	S	M	L	XL	XXL
To fit Bust (cm)	81-86	91.5-96.5	101.5-106.5	111.5-117	122-127
To fit Bust (in)	32-34	36-38	40-42	44-46	48-50
Actual Bust (cm)	86.5	96	106.5	116	126.5
Actual Bust (in)	34	37.8	42	45.8	50
Actual Length (cm)	57.5	59.5	61.5	63.5	65.8
Actual Length (in)	22.8	23.5	24.3	25	25.8

Note: Sleeve blocks to a looser gauge (20 rows per 10cm/4in) with 0.5cm/0.2in allowance at each end for dc edging

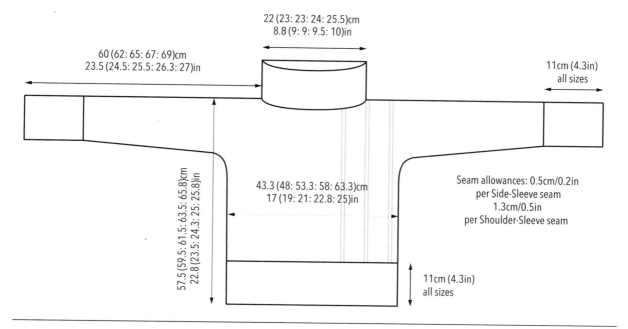

22 (23: 23: 24: 25.5)cm
8.8 (9: 9: 9.5: 10)in

60 (62: 65: 67: 69)cm
23.5 (24.5: 25.5: 26.3: 27)in

11cm (4.3in)
all sizes

57.5 (59.5: 61.5: 63.5: 65.8)cm
22.8 (23.5: 24.3: 25: 25.8)in

43.3 (48: 53.3: 58: 63.3)cm
17 (19: 21: 22.8: 25)in

Seam allowances: 0.5cm/0.2in
per Side-Sleeve seam
1.3cm/0.5in
per Shoulder-Sleeve seam

11cm (4.3in)
all sizes

INSTRUCTIONS

BACK

Near Side Lower Sleeve

With 3.5mm hook, ch35 (37: 41: 43: 45), turn.

Row 1 (RS) Ch2 (counts as 1 dc and 1 ch throughout), (1dc blo, ch1) in fifth ch from hook and in every alt ch to last ch, 1dc blo in last ch, turn. [35 (37: 41: 43: 45) sts]

Next 4 rows Work in main fabric patt to end, turn.

Row 6 (WS) Work in main fabric patt to end, cont with 2 ext ch, turn. [37 (39: 43: 45: 47) sts]

Next 7 rows Work in main fabric patt to end, turn.

Last eight rows form inc patt. Cont in inc patt as set for 48 (48: 48: 48: 48) more rows, turn. [49 (51: 55: 57: 59) sts]

Near Side Armhole Shaping

Row 1 (WS) Work in main fabric patt to end, cont with 4 ext ch, turn. [53 (55: 59: 61: 63) sts]

Row 2 Work in main fabric patt to end. [53 (55: 59: 61: 63) sts] Last two rows form new inc patt. Cont in new inc patt as set for 6 (6: 6: 6: 6) more rows, turn. [65 (67: 71: 73: 75) sts]

Bodice

Row 1 (WS) Work in main fabric patt to end, cont with 66 (70: 72: 76: 80) ext ch, turn. [131 (137: 143: 149: 155) sts]

Row 2 Ch2, (1dc blo, ch1) in fifth ch from hook and in every alt ch to next dc, (1dc flo, ch1) in each dc to last dc, 1dc flo in last dc, turn. [131 (137: 143: 149: 155) sts]

Next 25 (29: 35: 39: 43) rows Work in main fabric patt to end, turn.

Shape Neck and Remainder of Bodice

Row 1 (RS) Ch2, work in main fabric patt to third from last dc, 1dc flo in third from last dc, turn *(leave last 4 sts unworked)*. [127 (133: 139: 145: 151) sts]

Row 2 Work in main fabric patt to end, turn. ***

Row 3 Work in main fabric patt to second from last dc, 1dc flo in second from last dc, turn *(leave last 2 sts unworked)*. [125 (131: 137: 143: 149) sts]

Next 35 (37: 37: 39: 43) rows Work in main fabric patt to end, turn.

Next row (RS) Work in main fabric patt to end, cont with 2 ext ch, turn. [127 (133: 139: 145: 151) sts]

Next row Work in main fabric patt to end, turn.

Next row Work in main fabric patt to end, cont with 4 ext ch, turn. [131 (137: 143: 149: 155) sts]

Next 26 (30: 36: 40: 44) rows Work in main fabric patt to end, turn. **

Next row (WS) Ch2, (1dc flo, ch1) in fifth st from hook and in each of next 30 (31: 33: 34: 35) dc, 1dc flo in next dc, turn. [65 (67: 71: 73: 75) sts]

Far Side Armhole and Shoulder Shaping

Row 1 (RS) Work in main fabric patt to end, turn. [65 (67: 71: 73: 75) sts]

Row 2 Ch2, work in main fabric patt to third from last dc, 1dc flo in third from last dc, turn. [61 (63: 67: 69: 71) sts]

Last two rows form dec patt. Cont in dec patt as set for 6 (6: 6: 6: 6) more rows, turn. [49 (51: 55: 57: 59) sts]

Far Side Lower Sleeve

Rows 1-6 (starts with RS row) Work in main fabric patt to end, turn.

Row 7 (RS) Ch1, 1ss flo in third st from hook, (ss does not count as st, *PM in ss to avoid accidentally working into it at the end of next row*), (1dc flo, ch1) in next st *(which is a dc)*, and in each dc to last dc, 1dc flo in last dc, turn. [47 (49: 53: 55: 57) sts]

Next 7 rows Work in main fabric patt to end, turn.

Next row (RS) Rep Row 7. [45 (47: 51: 53: 55) sts]

STITCH CHART 1: FEATURE PANEL

A section of rows is shown to demonstrate patt reps and how sts line up if rows are worked straight.

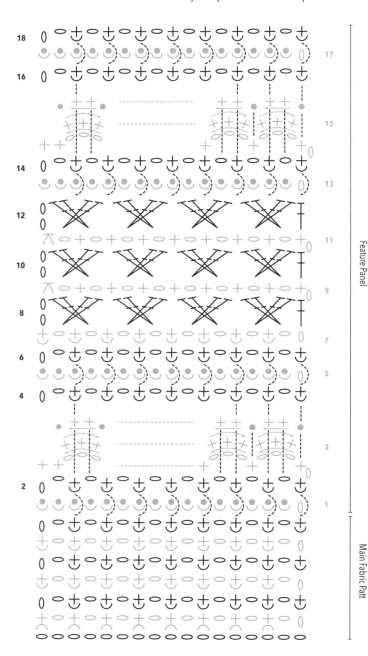

KEY

○	ch
+	dc
⌒	blo
⌣	flo
●	ss
⊤	tr
⋏	dc2tog
⤬	crossed-tr
	cable
	dotted line indicates to work st into aligned st 2 rows below

Last eight rows form new dec patt. Cont in new dec patt as set for 40 (40: 40: 40: 40) more rows, turn. [35 (37: 41: 43: 45) sts]
Next 6 rows Work in main fabric patt to end, turn.
Fasten off.

FRONT

Work as for back to ***.
Rep last two rows once, turn. [123 (129: 135: 141: 147) sts]
Next row (RS) Work in main fabric patt to second from last dc, 1dc flo in second from last dc, turn. [121 (127: 133: 139: 145) sts]
Next row Work in main fabric patt to end, turn.
Last two rows form new dec patt. Cont in new dec patt as set for 7 (7: 7: 7: 7) more rows, turn. [113 (119: 125: 131: 137) sts]
Next 13 (15: 15: 17: 21) rows Work in main fabric patt to end, turn. [113 (119: 125: 131: 137) sts]

Feature Panel and Shape Front Neck

Note: As you work following textured rows, crossed-tr rows will tend to splay wider and slant away at bottom edge. When you work subsequent ss and cable rows on other side of crossed-tr rows, it brings fabric back in line. Later, the bulk of added ribbings also helps to stabilise these edges. See Stitch Chart 1: Feature Panel and Special Abbreviations.
Row 1 (RS) Work ss row, turn. [113 (119: 125: 131: 137) sts]
Row 2 Work in main fabric patt into 2 rows below to end, turn.
Row 3 Ch1 (does not count as st), 1dc in st at base of ch, 37 (39: 41: 43: 45)cables, 1ss in dc worked in phase one of last cable made, 1dc in last st, cont with 2 ext ch, turn. [1 dc, 37 (39: 41: 43: 45) patt reps of cable, + 1 ss + 1 dc + 2 ext ch] *Note: St to be worked into after skipping 2 sts for each cable will alternate between being a ch or dc.*
Row 4 Ch2 (counts as 1 dc, 1 ch), (1dc flo, ch1) in fifth st from hook and in every alt st to last st, 1dc flo in last dc, turn. [115 (121: 127: 133: 139) sts] *Note: 'every alt st' will be a (dc; dc; ss) rep patt. Ss are identified by the diagonal bar angling down to right hand side every third st, which tends to crowd 2 dc between them, making dc immediately after ss easy to miss if you are not careful. See Stitch Chart 1 and study back of Row 3.*
Row 5 Work ss row, cont with 2 (4: 2: 4: 2) ext ch, turn. [117 (125: 129: 137: 141) sts]
Row 6 (Sizes S, L, XXL) Rep Row 2, turn. [117 (-: 129: -: 141) sts]
Row 6 (Sizes M, XL) Ch2 (counts as 1 dc and 1 ch), (1dc blo, ch1) in fifth ch from hook and rem of row as Row 2, turn. [- (125: -: 137: -) sts]
Row 7 Work in main fabric patt to end, cont with 4 ext ch, turn. [121 (129: 133: 141: 145) sts]
Row 8 Ch2 (counts as 1 tr), 30 (32: 33: 35: 36)crossed-tr working first rep into second and first ch-sps, 1tr in last st, turn.
Row 9 Ch1 (does not count as st), 1dc in st at base of ch, ch1, (skip 1 tr, (1dc, ch1) in next tr) to last 2 tr, dc2tog, cont with 4 ext ch, turn. [125 (133: 137: 145: 149) sts]
Row 10 Ch2 (counts as 1 tr), 31 (33: 34: 36: 37)crossed-tr working first rep into second and first ch-sps 1tr in last st, turn.
Row 11 Rep Row 9, turn. [129 (137: 141: 149: 153) sts]
Row 12 Ch2 (counts as 1 tr), 32 (34: 35: 37: 38)crossed-tr working first rep into second and first ch-sps, 1tr in last st, turn.
Row 13 Work ss row to last st, leave last st unworked, cont with 2 (0: 2:

0: 2) ext ch, turn. [131 (137: 143: 149: 155) sts]
Row 14 Work in main fabric patt into 2 rows below to end, turn.
Row 15 Ch1 (does not count as st), 1dc in st at base of ch, 43 (45: 47: 49: 51)cables 1ss in dc worked in phase one of last cable made, 1dc in last st, turn.
Row 16 Rep Row 4, turn. [131 (137: 143: 149: 155) sts]
Row 17 Work ss row, turn.
Row 18 Work in main fabric patt into 2 rows below to end, turn.
Row 19 (Sizes S, L, XXL) Ch2, dc2tog flo over fifth and sixth sts from hook, ch1, (1dc flo, ch1) in each dc to last 2 sts, dc2tog flo over last 2 sts, turn. [129 (-: 141: -: 153) sts]
Row 19 (Sizes M, XL) Work in main fabric patt to end, turn. [-: (137: -: 149: -) sts]
Row 20 Ch2 (counts as 1 tr), 32 (34: 35: 37: 38)crossed-tr, 1tr in last st, turn.
Row 21 Ch1 (does not count as st), 1dc in st at base of ch, ch1, (skip 1 tr, (1dc, ch1) in next tr) to last 2 tr, dc2tog, turn. [129 (137: 141: 149: 153) sts]
Row 22 Rep Row 20, turn.
Row 23 Rep Row 21, turn.
Row 24 Rep Row 20, turn.
Row 25 Rep Row 13, turn. [131 (137: 143: 149: 155) sts]
Row 26 Rep Row 14, turn.
Row 27 Rep Row 15, turn.
Row 28 Rep Row 16, turn.
Row 29 Rep Row 17, turn.
Row 30 Rep Row 18, turn.
Next 11 (15: 21: 25: 29) rows Work in main fabric patt to end, turn. Complete rem of front as for back from ** to end, do not fasten off, ch1 to change direction (does not count as st), cont with assembly instructions.

ASSEMBLY

Note: For all Row 1 edging across row instructions, insert hook under 2 lps into side of row end st.

EDGE FRONT LEFT SHOULDER-SLEEVE IN PREPARATION TO SEAM

Row 1 (RS) Working from cuff to neckline, work 1dc per row across the 81 (85: 91: 95: 99) rows from cuff to and including Row 30 of feature panel, 15 (15: 15: 15: 15)dc across the feature panel rows from end of Row 29 (ss row) to end of Row 13 (ss row), turn. [96 (100: 106: 110: 114) dc]
Row 2 (WS) Ch1 (counts as 1 dc), 1dc flo in third st from hook and in each dc to end, turn.
Row 3 Ch1 (counts as 1 dc), 1dc blo in third st from hook and in each dc to end. Fasten off.

EDGE BACK LEFT SHOULDER-SLEEVE IN PREPARATION TO SEAM, THEN COMPLETE SEAM

Row 1 (RS) Working from neckline to cuff, work 1dc per row across the 96 (100: 106: 110: 114) rows of main fabric, turn. [96 (100: 106: 110: 114) dc]
Rows 2-3 Rep Rows 2-3 top Front Left Shoulder-Sleeve, do not fasten

off, turn.

Ch1 (does not count as st), flat ss seam from cuff to neck, fasten off.

EDGE BACK RIGHT SHOULDER-SLEEVE IN PREPARATION TO SEAM

Row 1 (RS) Working from cuff to neckline, work 1dc per row across the 96 (100: 106: 110: 114) rows of main fabric, turn. [96 (100: 106: 110: 114) dc]

Rows 2-3 Rep Rows 2-3 top Front Left Shoulder-Sleeve, fasten off.

EDGE FRONT RIGHT SHOULDER-SLEEVE IN PREPARATION TO SEAM, THEN COMPLETE SEAM

As Edge Back Left Shoulder-Sleeve, ch1 (does not count as st), flat ss seam from cuff to neck, do not fasten off, cont to edge neckline and work ribbing.

EDGE NECKLINE

Edging round 1 (RS) Ch1 (counts as 1 dc in centre of right shoulder seam), working with RS facing around back of neckline, 3dc across rem shoulder seam rows, 48 (50: 50: 52: 56)dc across back of neckline to left shoulder seam, 7dc across left shoulder seam, 19 (19: 19: 19: 19) dc across feature panel neck shaping to Row 3 of feature panel, 14 (16: 16: 18: 22)dc across straight front neck rows, 19 (19: 19: 19: 19) dc across neck shaping, 3dc across rem shoulder seam rows, ss to first dc to join, turn. [114 (118: 118: 122: 130) dc]

Edging round 2 (WS) Ch1 (counts as 1 dc), 1dc flo in each dc around, including 12 evenly spaced dc2tog within round, ss to first dc, turn. [102 (106: 106: 110: 118) dc flo]

Next 13 rounds Work post tr ribbing, starting and finishing with RS rounds, maintaining 102 (106: 106: 110: 118) sts in each round, do not turn.

Next round (RS) Ch1 (does not count as st), (htr2tog blo, ch1) around, work secret sew finish.

Note: If any spaces within feature panel seem to gape where they meet neckline, use long tails to sew through sts around hole to reduce hole size before blocking.

****

EDGE LEFT SIDE-SLEEVE IN PREPARATION TO SEAM

Front Piece Left Side is already ready for seaming; join under lower sleeve of left front piece, edge RS underarm to cuff, ch1, edge RS left back sleeve-side to underarm then all the way to hem as folls:

Row 1 (RS) Insert hook in blo of second st below end of first left front sleeve row *(a dc)*, yoh and pull up lp, ch1 (counts as st), dc2tog over blo of next st *(a ch)* and side of dc (under 2 lps) at end of first sleeve row, (ch1, 1dc blo in next ch, ch1, dc2tog over blo of next ch and side of dc (under 2 lps) at end of next sleeve row) 4 times, *(stepped underarm now smoothed),* work 1dc per row (inserting hook under 2 lps) across rem 60 (60: 60: 60: 60) rows of left front sleeve to cuff. [78 (78: 78: 78: 78) sts]

Fold sleeve to cont edging RS of left back sleeve from cuff to underarm then to hem, ch1 (does not count as st), work 1dc per row (inserting hook under 2 lps) across 60 (60: 60: 60: 60) rows of left back sleeve, (dc2tog over end of next row (under 2 lps) and flo of next ch, ch1, 1dc

flo in next ch, ch1) 4 times, dc2tog over end of next row (under 2 lps) and blo of next foundation ch, (1dc blo, ch1) in next foundation ch and every second foundation ch to last foundation ch, 1dc blo in last foundation ch, turn. [142 (146: 148: 152: 156) sts]

Flat ss seam from hem to underarm to cuff. [142 (146: 148: 152: 156) ss]

Note: Sleeve is now an inside-out tube.

Cont with cuff edging.

EDGE CUFF

Edging round 1 (RS) Ch1 (does not count as st), 1dc blo in each st across sleeve [35 (37: 41: 43: 45) dc], 7dc across shoulder-sleeve seam, 1dc blo in each st across sleeve [35 (37: 41: 43: 45) dc], 1dc in sleeve seam row, ss to first dc to join, turn. [78 (82: 90: 94: 98) dc]

Edging round 2 (WS) Ch1 (counts as 1 dc), 1dc flo in each dc around, including 16 evenly spaced dc2tog within round, ss to first dc, turn. [62 (66: 74: 78: 82) dc]

Next 18 rounds Work post tr ribbing, starting with RS and ending with WS round, maintaining 62 (66: 74: 78: 82) sts in each round, turn; change to 3.25mm hook after first 6 rounds, then change to 3mm hook after first 12 rounds.

Next round (RS) Ch1 (does not count as st), (htr2tog blo, ch1) around, work secret sew finish.

Rep from **** for right side-sleeve and cuff.

EDGE HEM

Edging round 1 (RS) Join at lower side seam with a dc, work 1dc per row (under 2 lps) across main fabric of front and back, 1dc across each side seam, and 30dc across feature panel rows, ss to first dc to join, turn. [190 (210: 234: 254: 278) dc]

Edging round 2 (WS) Ch1 (counts as 1 dc), 1dc flo in each dc around, including 30 evenly spaced dc2tog within round, ss to first dc, turn. [160 (180: 204: 224: 248) sts] *Note: For a looser fit, omit decreases.*

Next 21 rounds Work post tr ribbing, starting and finishing with RS rounds, maintaining 160 (180: 204: 224: 248) sts in each round; change to 3.25mm hook after first 6 rounds, fasten off.

TO FINISH

Weave in all ends and block to measurements. See blocking and steaming guidelines on Nishio Sweater Pattern for best results.

QING XIN SWEATER
By Ana D
ana-d.com

MATERIALS
Scheepjes Namaste (50% Virgin Wool, 50% Acrylic; 100g/85m)
625 Scale x 5 (5: 6: 8: 10) balls
7mm crochet hook
8mm crochet hook

GAUGE/TENSION
6 ss with ch-2 sps in between and 12 rows to measure 10 x 10cm using an 8mm hook.
10 sts and 6 rows to measure 10 x 10cm over tr using a 7mm hook.

PATTERN NOTES
The sweater is worked top down in rows. It consists of 2 panels, front and back. The cowl is worked in rounds around neck opening after sweater assembly. Turn after each round to get same texture as waistband of sweater.

INSTRUCTIONS

PANEL (MAKE 2)
With 8mm hook, loosely ch102 (106: 112: 118: 122).
Row 1 (RS) Ss in fourth ch from hook (skipped ch counts as ch-2 sp), *ch2, skip 1 ch, ss in next ch; rep from * to end, turn. [50 (52: 55: 58: 60) ss, 50 (52: 55: 58: 60) ch-2 sps]
Row 2 (WS) *Ch2, ss in ch-2 sp; rep from * to end, turn. [50 (52: 55: 58: 60) patt reps of (ch2, ss in ch-2 sp)]
Rows 3-46 (48: 52: 54: 56) Rep Row 2. Fasten off at end of last row.
Skip 14 patt reps of (ch-2 sp, ss) and one more ch-2 sp, join yarn at ss.
Row 47 (49: 53: 55: 57) With 7mm hook, (working over next 20 (22: 24: 26: 26) patt reps only), ch3 (counts as 1 tr throughout), *1tr in ch-2 sp, 1tr in ss; rep from * to end, turn. [41 (45: 49: 53: 53) tr]
Row 48 (50: 54: 56: 58) Ch3, 1tr in each tr to end.
Rep last row 4 (4: 4: 5: 5) more times.

TO FINISH
For best results, block lightly before assembly. Place panels tog with WS facing out, sew shoulder seam over 19 (20: 21: 22: 23) ch-2 sps counted from side edge towards centre back on each side.

MEASUREMENTS
See Measurements Table

ABBREVIATIONS
See back cover flap

SCHEMATIC 1: GARMENT MEASUREMENTS

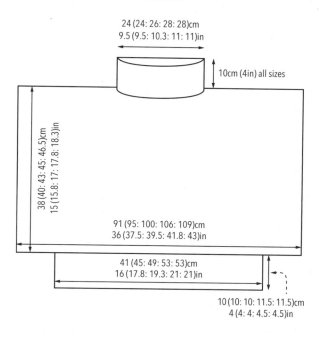

24 (24: 26: 28: 28)cm
9.5 (9.5: 10.3: 11: 11)in

10cm (4in) all sizes

38 (40: 43: 45: 46.5)cm
15 (15.8: 17: 17.8: 18.3)in

91 (95: 100: 106: 109)cm
36 (37.5: 39.5: 41.8: 43)in

41 (45: 49: 53: 53)cm
16 (17.8: 19.3: 21: 21)in

10 (10: 10: 11.5: 11.5)cm
4 (4: 4: 4.5: 4.5)in

You should have 12 (12: 13: 14: 14) ch-2 sps left to work for neck opening. Sew side edges of waistband and bottom edges of sleeves. Turn to RS. Weave in all ends.

COWL
Round 1 (RS) With 7mm hook, join yarn in ss at centre back of neck, ch3 (counts as 1 tr throughout), *1tr in ch-2 sp, 1tr in ss; rep from * around, ss to top of beg 3-ch to join, turn. [48 (48: 52: 56: 56) tr]
Round 2 (WS) Ch3, 1tr in each tr to end, ss to top of beg 3-ch, turn.
Rounds 3-6 Rep Round 2.

TO FINISH
Fasten off, weave in ends.

Measurements Table

Size	S	M	L	XL	XXL
To fit Bust (cm)	81	91.5	101.5	107	112
To fit Bust (in)	32	36	40	42	44
Actual Length from shoulder (cm)	48	50	53	56.5	58
Actual Length from shoulder (in)	19	19.8	20.8	22.3	22.8

OOLONG BLANKET
By Rachele Carmona
cypresstextiles.net

MEASUREMENTS
136 x 136cm (53.5 x 53.5in)

ABBREVIATIONS
See back cover flap

MATERIALS
Scheepjes Stone Washed XL (70% Cotton, 30% Acrylic; 50g/75m)
Yarn A: 851 Deep Amethyst x 23 balls
Yarn B: 872 Enstatite x 5 balls
6.5mm crochet hook
9mm crochet hook

GAUGE/TENSION
10 sts and 6 rows to measure 10 x 10cm over tr using a 6.5mm hook.

SPECIAL ABBREVIATIONS
2inc 1 st increased: 2tr in next st
3inc 2 sts increased: 3tr in next st
beg tr beginning treble crochet (counts as 1 tr): 1dc, ch1

PATTERN NOTES
Use Yarn A and 6.5mm hook for Panels, Joining and Border.
Use Yarn B and 9mm hook only for Surface Embroidery and tassels.
Panels are worked back and forth, therefore turn work after each row.
Skip 1 in the instructions means either skip 1 tr or skip ch-1 sp.

INSTRUCTIONS

PANEL 1 (MAKE 2)
Row 1 (RS) Ch25, 1tr in fourth ch from hook (skipped 3 ch count as 1 tr), 1tr in each ch to end, turn. [23 tr]
Row 2 (WS) Beg tr, 4tr, ch1, skip 1, 10tr, ch1, skip 1, 6tr. [21 tr, 2 ch-sps]
Row 3 Beg tr, 15tr, ch1, skip 1, 6tr. [22 tr, 1 ch-sp]
Row 4 Beg tr, 7tr, ch1, skip 1, 14tr.
Row 5 Beg tr, 11tr, ch1, skip 1, 10tr.
Row 6 Beg tr, 2tr, ch1, skip 1, 8tr, ch1, skip 1, 10tr. [21 tr, 2 ch-sps]
Row 7 Beg tr, 2tr, tr2tog, 3tr, ch1, skip 1, 9tr, ch1, skip 1, 4tr. [1 tr2tog, 19 tr, 2 ch-sps]
Row 8 Beg tr, 4tr, ch1, skip 1, 10tr, ch1, skip 1, 5tr. [20 tr, 2 ch-sps]
Row 9 Beg tr, 2tr, tr2tog, 10tr, ch1, skip 1, 6tr. [1 tr2tog, 19 tr, 1 ch-sp]
Row 10 Beg tr, 7tr, ch1, skip 1, 12tr. [20 tr, 1 ch-sp]
Row 11 Beg tr, 2tr, tr2tog, 5tr, ch1, skip 1, 10tr. [1 tr2tog, 18 tr, 1 ch-sp]
Row 12 Beg tr, 2tr, ch1, skip 1, 8tr, ch1, skip 1, 1tr, tr3tog, 3tr. [1 tr3tog, 15 tr, 2 ch-sps]
Row 13 Beg tr, 2tr, tr2tog, 8tr, ch1, skip 1, 4tr. [1 tr2tog, 15 tr, 1 ch-sp]
Row 14 Beg tr, 4tr, ch1, skip 1, 5tr, tr3tog, 3tr. [1 tr3tog, 13 tr, 1 ch-sp]
Row 15 Beg tr, 2tr, tr2tog, 3tr, ch1, skip 1, 6tr. [1 tr2tog, 12 tr, 1 ch-sp]
Row 16 Beg tr, 7tr, ch1, skip 1, 5tr. [13 tr, 1 ch-sp]
Row 17 Beg tr, 2tr, tr2tog, 9tr. [1 tr2tog, 12 tr]

Row 18 Beg tr, 12tr. [13 tr]
Row 19 Beg tr, 2tr, tr2tog, 8tr. [1 tr2tog, 11 tr]
Rows 20-25 Beg tr, 11tr. [12 tr]
Row 26 Beg tr, 2tr, ch1, skip 1, 4tr, 2inc, 3tr. [12 tr, 1 ch-sp]
Row 27 Beg tr, 7tr, ch1, skip 1, 4tr.
Row 28 Beg tr, 4tr, ch1, skip 1, 3tr, 2inc, 3tr. [13 tr, 1 ch-sp]
Row 29 Beg tr, 6tr, ch1, skip 1, 6tr.
Row 30 Beg tr, 7tr, ch1, skip 1, 1tr, 2inc, 3tr. [14 tr, 1 ch-sp]
Row 31 Beg tr, 2tr, 3inc, ch1, skip 1, 10tr. [16 tr, 1 ch-sp]
Row 32 Beg tr, 2tr, ch1, skip 1, 8tr, ch1, skip 1, 2inc, 3tr. [16 tr, 2 ch-sps]
Row 33 Beg tr, 2tr, 3inc, 9tr, ch1, skip 1, 4tr. [19 tr, 1 ch-sp]
Row 34 Beg tr, 4tr, ch1, skip 1, 10tr, 2inc, 3tr. [20 tr, 1 ch-sp]
Row 35 Beg tr, 13tr, ch1, skip 1, 6tr.
Row 36 Beg tr, 7tr, ch1, skip 1, 8tr, 2inc, 3tr. [21 tr, 1 ch-sp]
Row 37 Beg tr, 10tr, ch1, skip 1, 10tr.
Row 38 Beg tr, 2tr, ch1, skip 1, 8tr, ch1, skip 1, 5tr, 2inc, 3tr. [21 tr, 2 ch-sps]
Row 39 Beg tr, 7tr, ch1, skip 1, 9tr, ch1, skip 1, 4tr.
Rows 40-77 Rep Rows 2-39.
Rows 78-81 Rep Rows 2-5.
Row 82 Beg tr, 22tr. [23 tr]
Border Round
With RS facing, 3dc in first st of Row 82, 21dc, 3dc in last st of Row 82, 162dc evenly along row ends by working 2dc in side of next tr and each tr to end, 3dc in first st of Row 1, 21dc, 3dc in last st of Row 1, 162dc evenly along row ends as before, ss to first dc to join, fasten off.

PANEL 2 (MAKE 2)
Row 1 (RS) Ch23, 1tr in fourth ch from hook (skipped 3 ch count as 1 tr), 1tr in each ch to end. [21 tr]
Rows 2-6 Beg tr, 9tr, ch1, skip 1, 10tr. [20 tr, 1 ch-sp]
Row 7 Beg tr, 2tr, 2inc, 4tr, (ch1, skip 1, 1tr) 3 times, 3tr, 2inc, 3tr. [20 tr, 3 ch-sps]
Row 8 Beg tr, 7tr, (ch1, skip 1, 2tr) 3 times, 6tr.
Row 9 Beg tr, 2tr, 2inc, 3tr, (ch1, skip 1, 3tr) 3 times, 2inc, 3tr. [22 tr, 3 ch-sps]
Row 10 Beg tr, 6tr, (ch1, skip 1, 4tr) 3 times, 3tr.
Row 11 Beg tr, 2tr, 2inc, 1tr, (ch1, skip 1, 6tr) twice, ch1, skip 1, 1tr, 2inc, 3tr. [24 tr, 3 ch-sps]
Row 12 Beg tr, 2tr, 3inc, (ch1, skip 1, 8tr) twice, ch1, skip 1, 3inc, 3tr. [28 tr, 3 ch-sps]
Row 13 Beg tr, 2tr, 2inc, ch1, skip 1, 8tr, (ch1, skip 1, 1tr) 3 times, 7tr, ch1, skip 1, 2inc, 3tr. [28 tr, 5 ch-sps]
Row 14 Beg tr, 2tr, 3inc, 9tr, (ch1, skip 1, 2tr) 3 times, 7tr, 3inc, 3tr. [34 tr, 3 ch-sps]

Row 15 Beg tr, 2tr, 2inc, 10tr, (ch1, skip 1, 3tr) 3 times, 7tr, 2inc, 3tr. [36 tr, 3 ch-sps]

Row 16 Beg tr, 13tr, (ch1, skip 1, 4tr) 3 times, 10tr. [36 tr, 3 ch-sps]

Row 17 Beg tr, 2tr, 2inc, 8tr, (ch1, skip 1, 6tr) 3 times, 2tr, 2inc, 3tr. [38 tr, 3 ch-sps]

Row 18 Beg tr, 10tr, (ch1, skip 1, 8tr) 3 times, 3tr.

Row 19 Beg tr, 2tr, 2inc, 5tr, ch1, skip 1, 8tr, (ch1, skip 1, 1tr) 3 times, 7tr, ch1, skip 1, 5tr, 2inc, 3tr. [38 tr, 5 ch-sps]

Row 20 Beg tr, 7tr, ch1, skip 1, 9tr, (ch1, skip 1, 2tr) 3 times, 7tr, ch1, skip 1, 8tr.

Row 21 Beg tr, 5tr, ch1, skip 1, 10tr, (ch1, skip 1, 3tr) 3 times, 7tr, ch1, skip 1, 6tr.

Row 22 Beg tr, 15tr, (ch1, skip 1, 4tr) 3 times, 12tr. [40 tr, 3 ch-sps]

Row 23 Beg tr, 13tr, (ch1, skip 1, 6tr) 3 times, 8tr.

Row 24 Beg tr, 11tr, (ch1, skip 1, 8tr) 3 times, 4tr.

Row 25 Beg tr, 9tr, ch1, skip 1, 8tr, (ch1, skip 1, 1tr) 3 times, 7tr, ch1, skip 1, 10tr. [38 tr, 5 ch-sps]

Row 26 Beg tr, 2tr, tr2tog, 3tr, ch1, skip 1, 9tr, (ch1, skip 1, 2tr) 3 times, 7tr, ch1, skip 1, 3tr, tr2tog, 3tr. [2 tr2tog, 34 tr, 5 ch-sps]

Row 27 Beg tr, 4tr, ch1, skip 1, 10tr, (ch1, skip 1, 3tr) 3 times, 7tr, ch1, skip 1, 5tr. [36 tr, 5 ch-sps]

Row 28 Beg tr, 2tr, tr2tog, 10tr, (ch1, skip 1, 4tr) 3 times, 6tr, tr2tog, 3tr. [2 tr2tog, 34 tr, 3 ch-sps]

Row 29 Beg tr, 11tr, (ch1, skip 1, 6tr) 3 times, 6tr. [36 tr, 3 ch-sps]

Row 30 Beg tr, 2tr, tr2tog, 5tr, (ch1, skip 1, 8tr) twice, ch1, skip 1, 5tr, tr2tog, 3tr. [2 tr2tog, 32 tr, 3 ch-sps]

Row 31 Beg tr, 2tr, tr3tog, 1tr, ch1, skip 1, 8tr, (ch1, skip 1, 1tr) 3 times, 7tr, ch1, skip 1, 1tr, tr3tog, 3tr. [2 tr3tog, 26 tr, 5 ch-sps]

Row 32 Beg tr, 2tr, tr2tog, 8tr, (ch1, skip 1, 2tr) 3 times, 6tr, tr2tog, 3tr. [2 tr2tog, 26 tr, 3 ch-sps]

Row 33 Beg tr, 2tr, tr3tog, 5tr, (ch1, skip 1, 3tr) 3 times, 2tr, tr3tog, 3tr. [2 tr3tog, 22 tr, 3 ch-sps]

Row 34 Beg tr, 2tr, tr2tog, 3tr, (ch1, skip 1, 4tr) twice, ch1, skip 1, 3tr, tr2tog, 3tr. [2 tr2tog, 20 tr, 3 ch-sps]

Row 35 Beg tr, 4tr, (ch1, skip 1, 6tr) twice, ch1, skip 1, 5tr. [22 tr, 3 ch-sps]

Row 36 Beg tr, 2tr, tr2tog, 7tr, ch1, skip 1, 7tr, tr2tog, 3tr. [2 tr2tog, 20 tr, 1 ch-sp]

Row 37 Beg tr, 10tr, ch1, skip 1, 11tr. [22 tr, 1 ch-sp]

Row 38 Beg tr, 2tr, tr2tog, 6tr, ch1, skip 1, 6tr, tr2tog, 3tr. [2 tr2tog, 18 tr, 1 ch-sp]

Row 39 Rep Row 2. [20 tr, 1 ch-sp]

Rows 40-77 Rep Rows 2-39.

Rows 78-81 Rep Rows 2-5.

Row 82 Beg tr, 20tr. [21 tr]

Border Round

With RS facing, 3dc in first st of Row 82, 19dc, 3dc in last st of Row 82, 162dc evenly along row ends by working 2dc in side of next tr and each tr to end, 3dc in first st of Row 1, 19dc, 3dc in last st of Row 1, 162dc evenly along row ends as before, ss to first dc to join, fasten off.

PANEL 3 (MAKE 1)

Row 1 Ch45, 1tr in fourth ch from hook (skipped 3 ch count as 1 tr), 1tr in each ch to end. [43 tr]

Rows 2-62 Rep Rows 21-81 of Panel 2.

Rows 63-81 Rep Rows 7-25 of Panel 2.

Row 82 Beg tr, 42tr. [43 tr]

Border Round

With RS facing, 3dc in first st of Row 82, 41dc, 3dc in last st of Row 82, 162dc evenly along row ends by working 2dc in side of next tr and each tr to end, 3dc in first st of Row 1, 41dc, 3dc in last st of Row 1, 162dc evenly along row ends as before, ss to first dc to join, fasten off.

JOIN PANELS

Lay panels out in order 1-2-3-2-1. Panel 1 on left-hand side has Row 1 on RS. Panel 1 on right-hand side has Row 1 on WS. Hold 2 panels with WS tog and whip stitch tog using needle and Yarn A: attach yarn in one cnr and whip stitch along to end, making each st through both lps of aligned sts. Do not pull yarn to tighten sts; allow sts to rest flush against top edge of work. Rep for each panel.

WAVY STRIPES - SURFACE EMBROIDERY

With 2 strands of Yarn B held tog and 9mm hook, join yarn with ss between 3-tr group at edge of a panel and the next st (use photo as a guide). Make surface ch sts along edge of panels in between tr sts, making sure to keep 3-tr 'buffer' at edge.

Work each wavy stripe (8 in total) in same way from bottom edge to top edge of blanket, fasten off.

BLANKET BORDER

Rounds 1 and 2 (RS) Ss in top right cnr, (3dc in cnr, dc evenly across edge) 4 times, ss to first dc.

Round 3 Beg tr in cnr st, (4tr in same st, 1tr in each st across, 1tr in cnr st) 4 times omitting final tr, ss to beg tr.

Round 4 Beg tr in cnr st, *ch3, 1tr in same st, (ch1, skip 1, 1tr) across to next cnr st, ch1, skip 1, 1tr in cnr st, rep from * 3 times omitting final tr, ss to beg tr.

Round 5 (1dc, ch2, 1dc) in each ch-sp around, ss to first dc, fasten off.

TO FINISH

Weave in all ends.

Make 16 tassels with Yarn B: Cut 40 strands of 40cm each and fold through ch-1 sp of border aligning with end of wavy stripe. Wind yarn around folded strands to finish tassel.

JASMINE PONCHO WITH COWL

By Margaret Hubert
margaretshooksandneedles.blogspot.com

MEASUREMENTS
See Measurements Table

ABBREVIATIONS
See back cover flap

MATERIALS

Scheepjes Metropolis (75% Merino Extra Fine, 25% Nylon; 50g/200m)
056 Almaty x 8 (9: 10) balls for both Poncho and Cowl
4mm crochet hook
2 stitch markers

GAUGE/TENSION
3.5 shell patts and 9 patt rows to measure 10 x 10cm using a 4mm hook.

SPECIAL ABBREVIATIONS
shell (2tr, ch2, 2tr) in same st

PATTERN NOTES
There is no RS or WS to the poncho. The Front and Back are made in the same way and reversed when sewing up.

INSTRUCTIONS

PONCHO FRONT AND BACK
Ch147 (153: 159).
Patt Row 1 Shell in 6th ch from hook (skipped 5 ch counts as 1 dtr and 2 ch), *skip next 5 ch, shell in next ch; rep from * to last 3 ch, skip next 2 ch, 1dtr in last ch, turn. [24 (25: 26) shells, 2 dtr]
Patt Row 2 Ch2, 1dc in first dtr, *ch3, 1tr in next ch-2 sp, ch3, 1dc bet shells; rep from * to end, working last dc in top of turning ch, turn.
Patt Row 3 Ch4 (counts as 1 dtr throughout), skip next ch-3 sp, *shell in next tr; rep from * to last ch-3 sp, skip ch-3 sp, 1dtr in last dc, turn.
Cont to work Patt Rows 2 and 3 until piece measures 63.5 (66: 68.5) cm (25 (26: 27)in), ending with Patt Row 3.

First Shoulder Shaping
Next row Work Patt Row 2 until 3 (3: 4) shells are completed, turn.
Next row Work Patt Row 3, turn.
Rep last two rows once more, fasten off.
Second Shoulder Shaping
Skip centre 7 (8: 8) shells, join yarn in sp before next shell.
Next row Work Patt Row 2 to end, turn. [14 (14: 14) shells]
Next row Work Patt Row 3, turn.
Rep last two rows once more, fasten off.

SLEEVE (MAKE 1)
Ch57 (63: 69).
Row 1 Shell in sixth ch from hook (skipped 5 ch counts as 1 dtr and 1 ch), *skip next 5 ch, shell in next ch; rep from * to last 3 ch, skip 2 ch, 1dtr in last ch, turn. [9 (10: 11) shells, 2 dtr]
Row 2 Ch2, 1dc in first dtr, *ch3, 1tr in next ch-2 sp, ch3, 1dc bet shells; rep from * to end, working last dc in top of turning ch, turn.
Row 3 Ch4, skip next ch-3 sp, *shell in next tr; rep from * to last ch-3 sp, skip ch-3 sp, 1dtr in last dc, turn.
Rep Rows 2 and 3 once more, then Row 2 once.
Next row (inc) Ch4, 1dtr in first dc, *shell in next tr; rep from * to last ch-3 sp, skip ch-3 sp, 2dtr in last dc, turn. [2 sts inc]
Next row Ch1, 1dc in each of first 2 dtr, *ch3, 1tr in next ch-2 sp, ch3, **1dc bet shells; rep from * to last 2 dtr, ending last rep at **, 1dc in next dtr, 1dc in top of turning ch, turn.
Next row Ch4, 1dtr in next dc, *shell in next tr; rep from * to last ch-3 sp, skip ch-3 sp, 1dtr in each of last 2 dc, turn.
Rep last two rows once more.
Next row (inc) Ch1, 1dc in first dtr, 2dc in next dtr, *ch3, 1tr in next ch-2 sp, ch3, **1dc bet shells; rep from * to last 2 dtr, ending last rep at **, 2dc in next dtr, 1dc in top of turning ch, turn. [2 sts inc]

Measurements Table

Size	S	M	L
Actual Width flat (cm)	68.5	71.5	74.7
Actual Width flat (in)	27	28.3	29.3
Actual Length (cm)	68	70.5	73
Actual Length (in)	26.8	27.8	28.8
Sleeve Length (cm)	44.5	44.5	47.5
Sleeve Length (in)	17.5	17.5	18.8
Cowl Width (cm)	91.5	91.5	91.5
Cowl Width (in)	36	36	36
Cowl Height (cm)	37	37	37
Cowl Height (in)	14.5	14.5	14.5

SCHEMATIC 1: GARMENT MEASUREMENTS

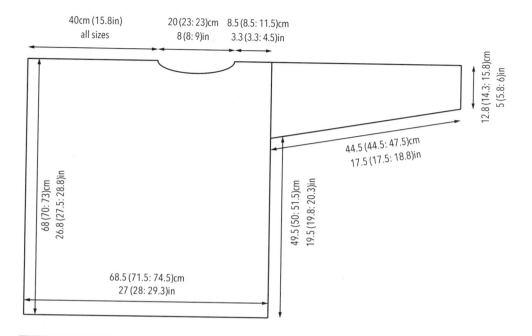

40cm (15.8in)
all sizes

20 (23: 23)cm
8 (8: 9)in

8.5 (8.5: 11.5)cm
3.3 (3.3: 4.5)in

12.8 (14.3: 15.8)cm
5 (5.8: 6)in

44.5 (44.5: 47.5)cm
17.5 (17.5: 18.8)in

68 (70: 73)cm
26.8 (27.5: 28.8)in

49.5 (50: 51.5)cm
19.5 (19.8: 20.3)in

68.5 (71.5: 74.5)cm
27 (28: 29.3)in

Next row Ch4, 1dtr in each of next 2 dc, *shell in next tr; rep from * to last ch-3 sp, skip ch-3 sp, 1dtr in each of last 3 dc, turn.
Next row (inc) Ch1, 1dc in first dtr, 2dc in next dtr, 1dc in next dtr, *ch3, 1tr in next ch-2 sp, ch3, **1dc bet shells; rep from * to last 3 dtr, ending last rep at **, 1dc in next dtr, 2dc in next dtr, 1dc in top of turning ch, turn. [2 sts inc]
Next row Ch4, 1dtr in each of next 3 dc, *shell in next tr; rep from * to last ch-3 sp, skip ch-3 sp, 1dtr in each of last 4 dc, turn.
Next row Ch1, 1dc in each of next 4 dtr, *ch3, 1tr in next ch-2 sp, ch3, **1dc bet shells; rep from * to last 4 dtr, ending last rep at **, 1dc in each of next 3 dtr, 1dc in top of turning ch, turn.
Rep last two rows once more.
Next row (inc) Ch4, skip 2 dc, shell in next dc, *shell in next tr; rep from * to last ch-3 sp, skip ch-3 sp and 1 dc, shell in next dc, skip 1 dc, 1dtr in last dc, turn. [11 (12: 13) shells, 2 dtr]
Next row Rep Patt Row 2.
Starting with first inc row, rep last 14 rows once more. [13 (14: 15) shells, 2 dtr]
Cont to work patt as set until sleeve measures 43 (43: 46)cm (17 (17: 18)in) ending with Patt Row 3, fasten off.

TO FINISH
Sew shoulder seams matching short ends tog (Left Shoulder) and long ends tog (Right Shoulder). PMs 18.5 (20: 21.5)cm (7.3 (7.8: 8.5)in) down from Left Shoulder seam on Front and Back for sleeve placement. Mark centre of sleeve top, pin sleeve in place with centre of top at shoulder seam and edges of sleeve at markers. Sew underarm of sleeve and Left side seam of Poncho.

SLEEVE CUFF
Join yarn at sleeve seam.
Round 1 1dc in base of each shell, 2dc in sp bet shells around, ss to first dc to join, do not turn.
Round 2 Ch1, 1dc in each dc around, ss to first dc, do not turn.
Round 3 Rep Row 2, fasten off.

BLOCKING
Place garment on padded surface, sprinkle with water, pull gently into shape, allow to dry. Do not press.

COWL (ONE SIZE)
Ch87.
Row 1 Shell in sixth ch from hook (skipped 5 ch counts as 1 dtr and 2 ch), *skip next 5 ch, shell in next ch; rep from * to last 3 ch, skip 2 ch, 1dtr in last ch, turn. [13 shells, 2 dtr]
Row 2 Ch2, 1dc in first dtr, *ch3, 1tr in next ch-2 sp, ch3, 1dc bet shells; rep from * to end, working last dc in top of turning ch, turn.
Row 3 Ch4 (counts as 1 dtr), skip next ch-3 sp, *shell in next tr; rep from * to last ch-3 sp, skip ch-3 sp, 1dtr in last dc, turn.
Cont to work Patt Rows 2 and 3 until piece measures 91.5cm (36in), fasten off.

TO FINISH
Sew short ends tog to form a ring, fold lengthwise so that one side is longer than the other by 5cm (2in), using photos as a guide. Fasten off, weave in ends. Blocking is not necessary for Cowl.

ORCHARD BLOSSOM HEADBAND
By Alia Bland
thelittlebee.co.nz

MEASUREMENTS
Length 56cm (22in), width 10cm (4in)
Measurements are adjustable,
see Pattern Notes

ABBREVIATIONS
See back cover flap

MATERIALS
Scheepjes Eliza (100% Polyester; 100g/230m)
Yarn A: 233 Pink Blush x 1 ball or Yarn B: 223 Soft Sage x 1 ball
Scheepjes Cahlista (100% Natural Cotton; 50g/85m)
Yarn C: 114 Shocking Pink x 1 ball
Yarn D: 385 Crystalline x 1 ball
Yarn E: 162 Black Coffee x 1 ball
Yarn F: 244 Spruce x 1 ball or Yarn G: 249 Saffron x 1 ball
5mm crochet hook
Washaway stabiliser or fabric chalk for embroidery (optional)

GAUGE/TENSION
Approx. 10 sts and 14 rows to measure 5 x 5cm over patt using
a 5mm hook.

SPECIAL ABBREVIATIONS
spike st work a regular dc into st one row below working row by
inserting hook into st and loosely pulling up lp to same height as
working row, complete st as normal

PATTERN NOTES
This headband is constructed from a long rectangle gathered at both
ends and sewn tog to create a band. A cover band is created from a
smaller rectangle and sewn around the join. Embroidery is stitched on
one side of completed headband.
Headband in Yarn A uses Yarns C, D, E and F for embroidery, headband
in Yarn B uses Yarns C, D, E, and G for embroidery. Instructions show
Yarn A colourway, with Yarn B colourway shown in brackets.
To ensure a good fit, ensure starting ch fits exactly around head circumference, adjust ch by adding or removing 2 sts at a time as necessary.

INSTRUCTIONS

MAIN BAND
With 2 strands of Yarn A (B) held tog (use outside and inside ends of
ball tog), loosely ch60, turn. *Note: See Pattern Notes to adjust length.*
Row 1 1dc in second ch from hook and in each ch to end, turn. [59 sts]
Row 2 Ch1 (does not count as st throughout), *1dc, spike st; rep from
* to last st, 1dc, turn.
Rows 3-14 Rep Row 2, fasten off after Row 14 leaving a 30cm tail.

COVER BAND
With 2 strands of Yarn A (B) held tog, loosely ch12, turn.
Row 1 1dc in second ch from hook and in each ch to end, turn. [11 sts]
Row 2 Ch1, *1dc, spike st; rep from * to last st, 1dc, turn.
Rows 3-5 Rep Row 2, fasten off after Row 5 leaving a 15cm tail.

JOINING
Gather end of Main Band (with yarn tail) into 3 small folds. Hold folds
tog or secure with a pin, and use tail to sew through folds widthways to
secure them. Cut yarn and use rem tail to repeat process at other end
of Main Band. Align two gathered ends tog and sew neatly tog to form
band. Fasten off, weave in ends.
Choose a RS and place Cover Band around Main Band join so that
edges meet in centre of WS. Use yarn tail to sew edges tog, sewing a
few sts into Main Band to secure. Fasten off, weave in ends.

EMBROIDERY
Choose left or right side of headband to embroider on to. Use
Embroidery Chart as a st guide. Either trace design onto washaway
stabiliser, trace with chalk or freehand sew.
Flowers and buds are created using 2 strands of yarn threaded
through tapestry needle, with ends matched evenly to make 4 strands
in total. Branch and leaves are created using a single strand, with ends
matched evenly to make 2 strands. Use 2 strands of Yarn C (D) to
embroider flowers 1, 2 and 3, using Lazy Daisy Stitch for petals.
Use 2 strands of Yarn D (C) to embroider centres of flowers 1 and 2,
using Bullion Stitch.
Use 1 strand of Yarn E to backstitch branches, and Bullion Stitch
underside of flower 3.
Use 1 strand of Yarn F (G) to embroider leaves, using Lazy Daisy Stitch.

TO FINISH
Double knot and trim all ends on WS at end. If using stabiliser, trim,
rinse off and dry flat.

SCHEMATIC 1: EMBROIDERY CHART

KEY

⌒⌒⌒ Back Stitch

))))) Bullion Stitch

◊ Lazy Daisy Stitch

Use Schematic 1: Embroidery Chart as a template to trace design. Chart shown is true to size 20 x 8cm (7.9 x 3.2in).

NOTES

NOTES